Praise for

All in

"*All In* is full of real-life, hard-won, street-smart lessons that are entirely applicable and transferable to any business."

—BERNIE MARCUS, Founder, Former Chairman & CEO The Home Depot

"In life, there are dreamers and doers. Bill Green lived his dream. And the experiential lessons he imparts are an inspiration for entrepreneurs"

—DAVID FALK, Founder & CEO FAME, Sports agent, who has represented some of the biggest names in pro basketball (including Michael Jordan) and Author of *The Bald Truth*

"It's great to read a book about business by an entrepreneur like Bill Green who really knows business. His life experiences will inspire readers to become successful entrepreneurs and prepare them to break through the barriers to grow and climb the ladder of success."

—TOM WOLF, Governor of Pennsylvania

"The idea of guiding a company from the minor to the big leagues of business can be exhilarating, but also daunting without a detailed set of directions. *All In* provides those directions with humility, comedy and street smarts."

—JOHN CALIPARI, Basketball Hall of Famer, National Championship Coach of the Kentucky Wildcats and *NY Times* Best Selling Author

"This book is a look at the mind of a savvy, street smart entrepreneur and will help you on your journey of building a successful business."

—MARTIN HANAKA, Former Chairman and CEO of The Sports Authority

"The Idea, the Team, the Customers– and, of course, the Entrepreneur. Most people have no idea what it really means, professionally and personally, to be an entrepreneur, much less to have repeatedly succeeded as one. Bill Green has, and in this book, he covers the journey from idea through sale and back again. If you're an entrepreneur, or aspire to be one, this book is well worth your attention."

—ROBERT WOLCOTT, Professor Of Innovation & Entrepreneurship, Kellogg School of Management at Northwestern University

"Bill Green takes readers on his delightful, humorous, and sometimes painful journey as a serial entrepreneur. Through engaging stories revealing valuable lessons that can't be learned in textbooks, aspiring entrepreneurs will discover that starting a business is the hardest work they'll ever do, but doing the work will reward them with a lifetime of opportunities."

—KATHLEEN ALLEN, Ph.D., Professor Emeritus, Lloyd Greif Center for Entrepreneurial Studies, Marshall School of Business, University of Southern California

"Bill Green's inspiring *All In* is not a book! It is the personal and intimate conversation between you, the reader, and the author who shares one of the most amazing and motivating journeys to success. If you want to succeed beyond your wildest dreams, PLEASE read and follow these 101 priceless lessons."

—DWIGHT CAREY, CEO American Productivity Group and Asst. Prof. of Entrepreneurship Temple University

"*All In* is a quick read with hands-on, practical advice from an accomplished entrepreneur who's cracked the code of success. Readers will laugh and nod as they consume creative lessons that can't be taught from a traditional classroom setting. Highly motivational and perfect for any savvy businessperson looking to grow his/her venture."

—JOEL SHULMAN, Ph.D., CFA, Professor of Entrepreneurship, Babson College

"Bill Green's *All In* is more than just a how-to guide for building a successful business. It's one man's story of how good, old-fashioned hard work, passion and great instincts created opportunities, then success and, most importantly, a great life."

—HOWARD ESKIN, sports anchor WTXF-TV "Fox 29" Philadelphia, sports radio personality WIP-FM 94.1/WTEL AM 610

"An amazing book that reveals the sometimes elusive insights that entrepreneurs need for success."

—RICHARD VAGUE, author of *Next Economic Disaster,* managing partner Gabriel Investments

"This is a great American success story of perseverance and overcoming adversity, to build a great business. The lessons Bill teaches are invaluable insights for people to become transformative entrepreneurs."

—JEFF BROWN, CEO Browns Super Stores

"*All In* is a Must Read for anyone with passion and courage who wants to find success and happiness."

—RON SUBER, President of Prosper Marketplace

"How refreshing! This book will enlighten true entrepreneurs! It is an absolute must-read for entrepreneurs who are serious about success."

—MITCHELL MORGAN, Founder, Chairman & CEO Morgan Properties

"Bill Green's *All In* brings to life the very essence of capitalism, demonstrating that hard work and ingenuity can pave the road to the American Dream. A must-read that will inspire young entrepreneurs."

—THOMAS MEYER, CEO Meyer Capital Group

"*All In* is an important book for anyone who is intent on building an meaningful business career. In simple terms, Bill describes how hope, desire, and a 'take no prisoners' attitude can lead to success beyond what most people can imagine."

—JEFFREY HARROW, Chairman, Sparks Marketing Group & Former CEO TravelOne

"I highly recommend this book to aspiring entrepreneurs. Buy it, use it and you will grow your business!"

—ROBERT POTAMKIN, Co-Chairman, Potamkin Automotive Group

"*All In* is more than a how-to guide, it's a 'how he did it' guide that should convince anyone thinking about starting a business that they don't need a fortune to start one."

—JOEL APPEL, Founder and Former CEO Global Furniture

"Love this book! All In is fun, real, high-energy, motivating, and inspiring."

—PAUL SILBERBERG, President of CMS Companies, Adjunct Professor Fox School of Business at Temple University

"Organized, driven, focused: all qualities that have enabled Bill Green to succeed in multiple business ventures. This book reflects who he is and why others can learn from his pearls of wisdom. I love Bill, not just for his business skills but for his thirst to succeed at whatever he attempts."

—SIDNEY BROWN, Chief Executive Officer, NFI Industries

"*All in* is a must read for all aspiring entrepreneurs! Bill's book is a road map to what to do and how to do it as well as and maybe the most important, what to stay away from and look out for!"

—IRA LUBERT, Co founder, Independence Capital Partners

"*All In* offers a roadmap to success, with humility, comedy, and street smarts."

—STAN MIDDLEMAN, Founder, Chairman & CEO Freedom Mortgage

"*All In* is proof that genius is truly 99% perspiration. Bill Green's humor and simple guideposts help keep one grounded and reminded that the road to success is made up of hard work, keeping an open mind, discipline and being nimble. As goods and services move increasingly faster, often eliminating human interaction altogether, Bill keeps us focused on keeping it simple and that human interaction with stakeholders, employees and customers always comes first."

—ALAN F. FELDMAN, CEO, Resource Real Estate and Professor at the Wharton School of the University of Pennsylvania.

All In:
101 Real-Life
Business Lessons for
Emerging Entrepreneurs

by Bill Green

ISBN 978-1-63393-466-5

Published by

 **köehlerbooks**™

210 60th Street
Virginia Beach, VA 23451
800-435-4811
www.koehlerbooks.com

All

101 REAL LIFE BUSINESS LESSONS
FOR EMERGING ENTREPRENEURS

in

BILL GREEN

VIRGINIA BEACH

CAPE CHARLES

For my first teachers and mentors,
my dear Mom and Dad.
You are the ones that put my foot on the right path
with love and life lessons.

Table of Contents

CHAPTER 1

I BELIEVE IN YOUR BIG DREAMS

Life is too short to be little.

—Benjamin Disraeli

I KNOW PEOPLE like you. You've got "that look" in your eye. It's a look of fierce determination. While all your friends are out having brunch, playing Pokémon GO, or doing yoga in their spare time, here you are reading a business book—and not just any book. You're reading my book because you've got dreams. Big ones. You're not just sitting around waiting for life to happen. You want to make things happen.

You're going somewhere.

I bet you already might own a profitable small business. That's awesome. Good for you; you're doing what you love. Maybe a lot of your friends already think you've "made it"— and why not? You're living the "American Dream." You're a successful entrepreneur with a nice house and a happy spouse— what else could you possibly want out of life?

Maybe you even have a business partner who says, "We've got a good thing going, why are you buying books about how to grow our business? Why rock the boat when the boat's sailing smoothly?" But something inside of you wants to rock it, right? You know deep down that your business could be so much more so you're reading my book because you're asking yourself, how can I get to the next level?

Am I in the ballpark?

I told you I know people like you. There's no shame in being ambitious. That is the essence of the real "American Dream." Where would we be without our big dreams? I don't know about anyone else in your life, but let me tell you, I believe in yours.

Who the heck am I, anyway? At my core, I'm just a scrappy kid who started his career "bootstrapping a startup" in the days before the word *startup* even existed. I built my first business from the ground up, out of one table at a flea market that eventually sold for $1.6 billion dollars.

I didn't get all that money myself! I only got a small fraction of it; somehow, I didn't get the memo to stick around for twelve more years. But talk about starting small.

If I can do it; I know you can too.

I WAS ONCE YOU

I will admit, I'm a sentimental guy. Growing up in the New Jersey suburbs the way I did, I wasn't born with a silver spoon in my mouth. I didn't come from a wealthy family. I certainly never went on any fancy vacations or attended any highbrow boarding schools. In fact, I never even graduated from college. Heck, I barely graduated from high school!

I was too busy building a business as a teenager to bother too much with homework or science projects. I'm what you call an "old-school" self-made man. No one gave me anything in life; I got my education in the real world where grades really counted—and boy, am I glad I did, because the insights I gained while "just doing it" have lasted me a lifetime.

My humble background is why I'll always have a soft spot in my heart for feisty entrepreneurs like you. Forty years ago, I was you. I was a small business owner who had a great idea for a business that I brought to life, and it was chugging along pretty well. I shouldn't have had any complaints. I was living the dream. But you know what? I had that same itch you do.

I didn't want to settle for good; I wanted great. Not just great, I wanted amazing. I didn't want to beat my competition. I wanted to own them.

Maybe you haven't been given anything. Maybe you didn't draw the luckiest lot in life. Neither did I. What's behind you is not important. No one will remember where you started. They'll only remember where you finish. Your dreams may seem like a fantasy to most people now, but if you combine a great idea with a lot of persistent and consistent hard work, you can get anything you want out of life.

Just look at me. I did it and along the way I learned 101 essential insights into making your business great that can be applied to virtually any business model on earth. These are the lessons I'm going to share with you. I didn't just wake up one day and have all these epiphanies. All these things I learned from experience. I had to make mistakes, I had to try again, I had to keep coming back day after day until I got it right.

I don't want you to make the same mistakes I did.

This book is a hybrid. I'm going to tell you my own story, not to gratify my ego, but because there are a lot of things I went through that might be useful for you to learn from.

In addition, I'm distilling some of the key learning experiences into those 101 essential insights I mentioned a moment earlier.

I hope you draw inspiration from my story, and I hope you take to heart the lessons I share.

If you've got the same drive I do, and I know you do, I want to show you how to conceive, build, and grow your business from a neophyte startup into a market-dominating company that provides amazing service, employs talented and motivated people, and attracts customers who don't just like you—they love you. They need you. They can't live without you.

Sound like fun? Sure it does!

A GREAT IDEA IS A POWERFUL WEAPON

Maybe you already had a business that failed. Hey, that's okay: you had to start somewhere. It may sound counterintuitive, but failing at something is an essential part of success. I bet you already have a great idea for a product or a business in your back pocket and don't know what to do with it. It feels good to own that idea, doesn't it?

A great idea is like gold in your hands. Nothing amazing ever happened from having a bad idea or no ideas at all. But a man or woman armed with a great idea? Forget about it. It's a powerful weapon.

I know you may not feel all that powerful right now. Some days it seems like it's you against the world, right? Do some people's eyes glaze over when you pitch them your concept at a dinner party or when you're at your kid's soccer game? I hate it when that happens. But it does, even to the best of us. Forget those guys. Stay focused. Don't let anyone tell you that your dreams are irrelevant. They'll be the first to brag that "they knew you way back when" once you do make it.

Know this: it doesn't cost anything not to believe in something. It costs everything to believe in an idea so much that you're willing to spend your life doing it and doing it until it becomes a reality. That's guts. That's passion. That's the resolve you need to succeed. If anyone tells you a little guy with a great idea can't make it in this economy—that only rich guys or tech kids from Silicon Valley can get their ideas funded—just let it roll off your shoulders. Those naysayers don't have your vision.

They don't have your unbending intent.

WHY LISTEN TO A GUY LIKE ME?

I certainly didn't let anyone stop me from achieving my dream. I started working flea markets with one of my buddies when I was seventeen. Then my buddy dropped out and it was just me, until one day when a lucky kind of disaster struck at home.

My dad, Marty, lost his job after twenty-eight years.

Overnight, I had become the only breadwinner in the family. My dad saw what I was doing and said, "I'll tell you what, I'll help you at the flea markets while I look for work."

Suddenly, I had a partner again.

Dad and I worked the flea markets around Philadelphia and New Jersey six days a week and turned selling hardware and plumbing supplies into a profitable flea-market business. A year later, we turned that into a hardware store, all before I was out of high school.

Once we had the hardware store up and running, my dad was back to making the same salary he had at his old job. He was happy again. He'd see me plotting world domination, and he'd say, "Billy, why rock the boat? We're comfortable."

Sound familiar? I wasn't satisfied. I didn't want to end up like Richie Cunningham on *Happy Days*, working at my dad's hardware store all my life, even though I was the co-owner of the business. Just the thought of it drove me nuts, so I was motivated to think long and hard about getting bigger. Dad (love him to death) didn't have the vision I had. He had dropped out of high school when he was sixteen. My mom, who was now part of the family business, felt as Dad did. She had been supposed to go to the Juilliard School of Music, but her father wouldn't let her because girls were supposed to get married and have babies.

Those were the times we lived in.

So there I was, alone with my ambition. I spent many nights thinking about how I could expand our business into something more. Then one day, Dad and I came up with an idea: why didn't we offer credit accounts to commercial clients like apartment buildings? We knew of hardware stores back in Brooklyn who were doing it. Why not us? That's got a bigger upside, right? So we created a specialized niche market in our area by distributing to customers on commercial credit accounts. With that one move, we went from a small neighborhood hardware store to a wholesale distribution business called Wilmar (short for William and Martin), and we were off to the races.

Fast-forward to almost twenty years later. I had bought Dad out of the business long ago, and he and Mom were retired and living more comfortably than they ever could have imagined. I won the 1996 Delaware Valley Entrepreneur of the Year award, sponsored by Ernst and Young, NASDAQ, and *USA Today*.

Later that year, Wilmar went public (NASDAQ: WLMR).

Forbes magazine rated Wilmar as one of the "Best IPOs of 1996," and in 1999 *Forbes* named it one of the "200 Best Small Companies in America." It was a pretty good time in my life. Most people in my shoes would have been content.

I wasn't.

After the IPO, the business was thriving, but I kept thinking bigger. I looked at how fragmented the industrial distribution marketplace was, and I thought, *all these companies we're competing against really should be under one umbrella . . . we'd operate better as a whole, be more profitable, and provide a better client experience.* I didn't wait for some other company to get the same idea. I didn't wait to be acquired. I started acquiring our competitors one by one. We acquired and integrated over fifteen companies from 1996 to 2001, and got so big that we changed our corporate name from Wilmar Industries to Interline Brands.

In some cases, we left the existing core brand names of the companies we acquired in place for all sales and marketing functions. Interline was the umbrella corporation that never touched customers, so they never had to change who they did business with. I sound like a pretty smart guy in this instance, right? Let me tell you, I had to make a mistake to learn this lesson too. We tried to integrate our first acquisition without keeping their brand in front of their existing customers, and it was a mess. This is how you learn: by making mistakes.

For twenty-five years, I kept learning, adjusting, building, and acquiring, and you know what? It turned out pretty well. I led Wilmar-Interline from a small retail outlet to an industry-leading $630 million distribution business with 2,300 employees and 60 distribution centers across the United States, Canada, and Puerto Rico. As CEO, I personally managed the company's banking and institutional shareholder relationships. I've always had a talent for sales and marketing, so I also kept a hands-on role in the day-to-day operations of the company. I was a pioneer in the catalogue market as well as using technology to improve our processes. I integrated the latest tech into our distribution and customer service operations way before the Internet ever existed. And man, did it work. It's still working today. Interline Brands has revenues of over $1.8 billion and is owned by The Home Depot.

That's a lot of hardware.

BUT THAT'S NOT THE END OF THE STORY

For a lot of people, this would have been enough, right? After I sold my stake in Interline, I had enough money to live comfortably for the rest of my life. I tried to retire for a couple of months, but that's not who I am.

I still had that itch.

I was only forty-three and couldn't imagine sitting around playing golf all day for the rest of my life, so I started thinking about what I could do next.

Something different. Something big.

I didn't want to be known just as an industrial distribution expert, so I thought about how I could expand my skills into other areas and got interested in private equity. I founded WSG Partners, LLC (now known as Crestar Partners), a boutique co-investment private equity firm where I shared my knowledge and experience with all types of business entrepreneurs who were looking for partners. I invested in some pretty cool companies in a wide array of markets (like fitness clubs, a coffee company, a cigar company, a vendor management company, a specialty liquor line, and even a safety and homeland defense supply company).

From 2003 to 2008, WSG Partners made equity investments in nine privately held businesses. I participated with other private equity firms that did management-led buyouts, recapitalizations, strategic minority equity investments, and growth capital financing. I wasn't just an equity partner; I was an active investment participant who got involved when they needed me, way beyond the board-of-directors level. I enjoyed mentoring CEOs and even challenged them when necessary. I wasn't afraid to go all in when I believed in something.

Then, in 2008, I switched gears again. I wanted to expand my game even further, so I created Crestar Capital, and got into the tax lien business. We acquired more than 45,000 liens in excess of $300 million in lien value and more than $2 billion in asset value. I parlayed that experience in 2012 to create Crestar Homes, which acquires, renovates, sells, and leases previously owned homes. To date, Crestar has owned and managed more than 430 properties.

But I wasn't finished yet. I kept building off the new knowledge and skills I'd acquired. I never stayed still; I kept evolving and expanding my reach. I was frustrated with the process of financing my own real estate, so I thought, *Why don't I capitalize on my underwriting and finance experience and get into real estate finance?* So I founded the company LendingOne in 2014, a fintech (financial technology) company that provides one-year loans for "fix-and-flip" projects and long-term rental loans to nonowner-occupied real estate investment projects. My newest creation is going great. I'm confident it's going to be a $1 billion a year originator. It's just a matter of how long it's going to take to get there.

Would you bet against me?

I wouldn't bet against you either.

COLLEGE CAN BE A DOUBLE-EDGED SWORD

As you can see, I've done a lot of different things in my life. You name it, I've either done it or spent time thinking about how I could get involved. I've had success in a lot of different industries and even a few failures. So I'm not some know-it-all with a silver-bullet business solution that's going to turn your goose gold and send you to the top of the NASDAQ overnight. Newsflash: that guy with the silver bullet doesn't exist. I'm not that smart. I'm just a curious, determined person who knows how to adapt to the changing times and compensate for my shortcomings. I learned all I know on the street, talking to clients, knocking on doors, and pounding the pavement. You don't need an MBA to do what I do.

You may think I'm advocating against going to college, but I don't want to give you that impression. I'm not going to tell you college is worthless, because I believe you should have an education. But these days, if you look around, you'll see there is a college debt epidemic in the United States. I see kids (or their parents) spending a hundred grand or two hundred grand on a college education. Do you know how long you're going to have to work to pay all that off? Put a pencil to paper, and it might give you pause.

To make matters worse, a lot of these kids get out of college with a fancy degree from an elite school and guess what? They can't find a good job. Some can't even find a job in their field of study. Why? Because the Mark Zuckerbergs of the world have already snatched them up! For all the kids who go to college, there is a whole generation of people who got in at the ground level of a company and worked their way up. And don't forget the people who already came up with their great ideas and busted their butts to implement them while all the college kids were theorizing over widgets in class. This has left a whole lot of educated young adults scratching their heads. Not only are they behind their competition in work experience—they're also saddled with all this debt.

I hear from a lot of young people who are second-guessing their decision to go to school. They ask me for advice and I say, If you're struggling with whether it's worth it to spend all that money on a piece of paper or put that money into your own business, I can't tell you what the right answer is for you. I've seen successful people come from both worlds. If you want to start a robotics company or become a rocket scientist—you probably need to go to college! But if you're a young aspiring entrepreneur reading this book, you probably want to be a small business owner in a field that doesn't take years to understand. Now, this is where I can give you some advice based on my short-lived college experience.

The year was 1977. The hardware store business was going pretty well, but I still wanted to give college a shot. My dad didn't understand. He said, "Go ahead," but he didn't care either way. Back in those days, I was probably the only salesman who told their customers, "Don't call me before noon, because I'm getting an education." So I'd show up for my classes in a suit. That was considered weird back then (I'm sure it still is), but I had to wear one because I went to work after school. So one day I was in my Introduction to Business Management class, and the management teacher stopped me and said, "You come to school in a suit?"

I explained, "I have a business with my dad. After class, I leave school to go sell to clients."

My teacher asked me, "Would you mind speaking to my sales class?"

I said, "Sure."

Then I asked the teacher what he did prior to becoming a professor, and he said he owned a store on the Ocean City boardwalk in New Jersey. I knew those stores: they were about half the size of a closet! That was small potatoes stuff. Needless to say, I was not impressed, but I spoke to his sales class anyway.

A few days later, I had an epiphany while I was talking to his class. I looked at all the kids out there listening to me speak who all had dreams of making it big. Then I looked at the teacher and thought, *Wait a minute. How could this guy who sold trinkets on the Ocean City boardwalk teach me anything about business management?* I wanted to be way bigger than having a little store on the boardwalk. Heck, the business I was already running was way bigger than the biggest store this guy ever managed. And that's when it all started to come together. I said to myself, *I'm working my butt off all the time so I can pay for these classes, which take a little more than nothing to pass. Why do I need school? I'm wasting my time.*

So I quit college. Do I have any regrets? That's a tough one. How could I have any regrets with my business career? That turned out great, but I will say deep down that not getting a college education was a life experience that I sorely miss. I wish I had done it, but I wouldn't change a thing.

STILL, I HAD A THIRST FOR KNOWLEDGE

Instead, I sought my education elsewhere. I studied on my own. I read books. I found mentors who could teach me the things I needed to know. I remained inherently curious about how things worked, so I asked questions. Lots of them. I developed a personal thirst for knowledge to compensate for my lack of formal education. I kind of had a chip on my shoulder about it; I wanted to prove to the world that you didn't need an MBA to make it. And it worked for me.

When I got Wilmar going strong, I wanted to pass down my drive for self-improvement to my employees. I wanted to instill in all my sales force the same edge to achieve that I had. So I offered "continuing education courses" way before it was the norm for companies my size. I wasn't able to pay for all my employees to go to college, but I did what I could. I had guys from Dale Carnegie come in and speak to our sales team on Saturdays. They were masterful at teaching my sales force Salesmanship 101.

We also created the Wilmar Internal Library. It was set up in a giant display case in our lunchroom and was full of self-improvement tapes that we encouraged our employees to check out. We had every kind of sales and self-improvement tape imaginable—from Stephen Covey to Ken Blanchard. We had some really cool stuff.

I would tell my sales team: "Look, guys, you don't have to be a born salesperson to be great. If you're in your car for eight hours a day, and many of you are, I highly encourage you to listen to these self-improvement tapes and hone your game. You didn't go to Harvard. So what? Think of this as your 'rolling university.' There's so much training for salespeople out there if you want it. But you have to want it."

I didn't stop there. When I happened to be riding in one of my salespeople's cars, I would get on their case if they were listening to sports radio. I'd say, "C'mon, you're wasting your time. Why not work on improving your fastball instead of listening to a bunch of millionaires improve theirs? Don't you want to be a millionaire too?"

It didn't take long for my salespeople to turn off WIP Sports Radio whenever I got in their cars! They knew what I was up to when I asked them for a ride to the next customer meeting. But I know it worked with a lot of guys too. A lot of my salespeople thanked me for giving them those subtle kicks in the rear, because it motivated them.

A LIFETIME OF BUSINESS EXPERIENCE IN ONE BOOK

I want to give you the knowledge you need to succeed as well as that extra push to take your game to the next level. I want to be your paperback mentor, because I think you've got what it takes. You're going to need a lot of people like me giving you advice if you're going to make it, trust me. You'll have to take your lumps like the rest of us, but hopefully you'll learn how to avoid some of the most common business mistakes by learning how a guy like me navigated my way through it.

I can't guarantee you a 100 percent success rate. A lot of things will have to fall right for anyone to be a hit in this life (there are these things called timing, opportunity, and luck). But I can guarantee you will be a lot better equipped to grow your business with smarts, so that one day, if the stars align like they did for me—you'll be hitting so many home runs that the big boys are going to take notice.

What's that old saying? *Don't look a gift horse in the mouth?* Most CEOs who have had a lot of success won't tell you their tricks. Why? They want to keep their trade secrets secret. They don't want more competition. They want no competition! That's why they call it the "Good Old Boys Club."

But not me. I've never been in that club, but I'm going to help you storm the castle. I'm going to let you in on many of the tricks I learned in my career, and it's not going to cost you anything except what you paid for this book. I'm going to show you how to think, act, and manage your business like a real *Shark Tank*-worthy "Entrepreneur of the Year" and prepare you to waltz into that next investor meeting so you can find the financial backing you need to grow your business while reducing your personal risk.

And when you're finally cruising along like that fine-tuned foreign automobile you've always wanted to own, I'll tell you how to go about acquiring your competitors so you can take your company public and parlay your success into any other business venture you can dream of.

Sound like some serious fun? All right then, fasten your seatbelts; let's rev it up. This is going to be an inspiring and fun ride.

CHAPTER 2

WHAT CAN YOU CONTROL THAT IS FREE?

I have no special talents. I am only passionately curious.

—Albert Einstein

THERE'S THIS STORY about Hall of Fame NFL football coach Bill Parcells. He's a New Jersey guy you may have heard of—he won a few Super Bowls for the New York Giants. He used to walk around and individually tell his players to "get your expectations up" before every season. It didn't matter how good the player was or how talented that particular team was, he'd preach it to everyone from the quarterback to the water boy. What's the benefit of having high expectations for yourself? No team can win the Super Bowl unless everybody believes it. The same goes for building a successful business. No one is going to believe in your big idea or your leadership unless you believe it yourself.

From now on, I want you to expect great things from yourself and your business. Make it your daily mantra. I don't just want you to believe; I want you to be so confident in your success that others can feel your enthusiasm and visualize your "big dream" when you're talking. You gotta ooze passion out of every pore in your body. The whole world may think you're nuts, but if you know it's true, you've got a shot. The world may not always meet you halfway, but if you keep stretching out to cross the goal line and believing you're going to make it, then one day, you're going to score the game-winning touchdown.

That was one of Coach Green's pep talks; I gotta keep you guys into it! You ready to run through a wall to make your business soar? You ready to learn my secret playbook? Fantastic.

"WHAT'S FREE IN LIFE?"

I posed this question to my class a few years ago, when I was a guest professor at Rutgers University. They asked me to speak to their business school so I said, *What the heck.* A few days before my first class, I had a crisis of confidence. What was I going to teach these kids? I thought about it and said to myself, *Let's teach them some things they can use in life and some things they can take with them as they move on in their career.*

I titled my PowerPoint presentation, "It's Free." Then I got up in front of my class and posed this question to my students, "What can you control that is free? You can't control whether you were born into wealth or poverty. You can't control whether you are able to pay for a great college or no college. You can't control whether you were born with intelligence, looks, charisma, or humor—but there are so many things in life that you can control, so many things that anyone can do, no matter who you are. These are commonsense things that are easy to replicate, and the best part is they don't cost you a dime to implement into your routine."

I remember one of the kids remarked, "What industry are you talking about exactly?"

I said, "Good question. It doesn't matter. These things can be applied to any business and accomplished by any person as they move through life."

I've worked in some complex business arenas on some pretty involved scenarios in my career, so instead of diving into the deep end right off the bat, I want to do the same thing I did with my Rutgers class and get your feet wet first.

Let's begin with the most basic, fundamental business plays in my playbook that anyone can accomplish. If you can master these basic rules, then you'll be two steps ahead of a lot of business owners who may have a great idea going but don't know jack about how to do the small stuff right.

1: ALWAYS BE ON TIME

This may sound like a no-brainer, but if you want to achieve any serious goal in life—always be on time! I know it's cool to show up casually late to a party or whatever, but I'm talking about serious appointments, big-dream stuff. I learned this lesson pretty early on as a kid, and it stuck with me throughout my career. It's part of being a professional, and it's an easy thing to make part of your routine. It shows your customers and business partners that you have integrity. It shows that you can be trusted. It shows that you care about their time. It shows that you are impeccable with your word and when you say something, you mean it.

Be on time to everything. Be early if you have to. I don't want to hear any excuses. Traffic was a doozy? So what? That's like someone saying, "My dog ate my homework." That's why they call it "rush hour." Assume it's going to be horrific and leave even earlier. What's that old saying, "The early bird gets the worm?" It's true in the animal kingdom and true in the business jungle. You want to eat? You get there first. You want a customer's business? Guess who has the best chance to get it. Most of the time, it's the first person that shows up.

If a customer calls and wants to see me at nine o'clock in the morning, you can bet I'm going to be there ten minutes early. Unless there's a natural disaster going on within two hundred feet of the office, five after is unacceptable. So be on time. It's important. And it costs you nothing.

You might be wondering why I'm starting this book with advice that is so obvious. Well, if it were obvious, I wouldn't have to mention it! The reality is that most people are very casual with the time of people who are important to them, or should be important to them.

I'm talking about prospects, customers, bosses, coworkers, and family and friends.

Shakespeare said that promptness is the courtesy of kings. It's the courtesy we owe everyone in our lives. And if you aren't planning on showing up on time for client calls, meetings, or other essential moments on your calendar, there's really no point in reading the rest of the book!

2: BE POSITIVE AND SMILE

Who wants to be around unhappy people? You may love someone enough to do it in your personal life, but the same sympathy doesn't apply in business. No one wants to work with people who have bad attitudes. So maybe you're at work one day, and you feel lousy. Your spouse is mad at you and your kids are not speaking to you. Hey, look on the bright side. It could be worse. You're living in the 21st century. No bears are trying to eat you and you're not dying from smallpox. So smile. At least you still have your job, your health, and a family to be mad at you—so why poison other people's day with your bad vibes?

Being nice is so easy to do, and so many people don't even attempt it these days. It's like being "unimpressed" is the new cool thing to do, but it's sure not when you're trying to land a new customer. It's crazy to say, but smiling has become a lost art. So few people have face-to-face meetings any more, people are forgetting some of the most basic rules of civility.

Have you ever done business with a "classic" New Yorker who had that classic New York attitude? You go into a sandwich shop, and one of the guys behind the counter says, "Yo! What you wanna order?" Unless you're an eccentric genius like the Soup Nazi on *Seinfeld* or a rock-star chef like Gordon Ramsay, being rude is not a winning recipe for making raving fans of your work. Picasso could insult people who bought his paintings, but you're not Picasso. So smile when dealing with your clients.

Be nice to everybody, and I mean everybody, all the time. You'll be amazed how important "gatekeepers" like receptionists, secretaries, and assistants are to your success. You saw the movie *Wall Street*, right? How did Bud Fox get in to see Gordon Gekko? He buttered up his secretary. Be like Bud. Be nice to all gatekeepers. Ask them how they are. They love that kind of human engagement; it brightens their day. Do it right, and I guarantee they will become your ally.

Same goes for the people who are second in charge. Be nice to them too. One day you'll go into a business meeting and realize the person who was just a peon last week has suddenly become the boss. Thank God you treated that guy or gal with respect!

I've found even the most difficult business negotiations benefit from an injection of humor—everything does. It's the way we humans cope. We laugh about the difficult things we have to go through, because it keeps us sane.

I'm not talking about just smiling during in-person meetings. I want you to do it all the time, even when you're on the phone. They can hear you smiling through the phone; I'm serious! Your voice sounds different. You sound like you want to be there. One of my pet peeves is when I call in to a customer-service hotline and get reps that clearly hate their job. You know what I'm talking about. These people are not smiling. They are unhelpful and unfriendly, and often speak their "script" in a robotic fashion, wanting to get off the phone as soon as possible so they can get back to being miserable. It's depressing to get someone like that, right?

I wanted to make sure that never happened at Wilmar, and was so adamant about wanting our customer service reps to smile when they were on the phone that I thought about ways to help them do it. I didn't want their managers walking around and forcing people to smile, so I thought of a different option. Everyone looks better when they are smiling, right? So I installed mirrors that said, "Smile and Dial" in the workstations of all our reps to remind them to smile—and it worked. Hey, look how nice you look when you smile. People got it. Life is just better when you're being positive and treating people the right way. So smile already.

3: RETURN CALLS IN LESS THAN 24 HOURS

Do you know how many times I've heard customers complain, "It took them three days to call me back?" Man, that's just rude, right? You want my business and you won't even call me back?

It drove me crazy to hear this, so I told all my people: No one wants to feel like they have been left blowing in the wind. If you want their business, you better be responsive. Call customers back within twenty-four hours, no matter what. If you're having a baby, put your "out of office reply" on your email and voicemail telling them, "I'm going to be out of the office, and this is when I will return."

I was so passionate about it, I went to what some CEOs might categorize as extreme measures to pass it down to my employees. I led by example! When I was running Wilmar, I had a personal 800 number installed in my office just for customers. Then I created a business card just for them with my 800 number on it. I didn't have my calls screened by a computer or by my administrative assistant. It was just me. If I was in my office and the phone rang, I'd pick up and say, "Bill Green speaking. What can I help you with?" It was no publicity stunt. I sincerely wanted to help any customer at any time. And when I was out of the office, I tried to return everybody's call in less than twenty-four hours.

That idea may seem crazy today when no one talks on the phone anymore, but it doesn't always have to be a returned phone call. That's why I love email, because you can respond via email much faster than a call. If you can't call a client back immediately—email them personally. Even if it's two in the morning and the client is asleep, assure them that you received their call and will respond to their request at a certain time.

This may sound like a small thing, but being consistently responsive to clients builds trust. I wanted my customers to know through our actions that even though our company was growing fast, we were still a "neighborhood store" at heart who really cared about them. That builds loyalty. I will get into this later, but a big part of fostering an army of raving fans is forging an emotional connection with your customers. Responding to their calls shows that you're there for them and is a great way to keep them coming back.

At LendingOne, whenever a prospect "almost completes" a loan application online, we strive to call them back within an hour, and in many cases, we get back to them within minutes.

That kind of response time builds customer loyalty.

4: FIND A MENTOR

You already know what you want to do with your business, right? So look at the marketplace, and target some players in your business area that you aspire to be like. Is there someone in your network who's doing what you want to be doing one day? If so, reach out to them. You don't have to walk up and say, "Will you be my mentor?"—just establish a relationship and ask for advice.

A mentor can be any person that has skill, experience, or expertise in an area that could help your career. Usually it's information you can't learn in books or online, so it's vital that you pick his or her brain to get that "intel." You'll be surprised how responsive successful people can be. You'll find many people are flattered that you are asking for their advice, so they will help you. And that's what you need if you're going to make it in the real world—help, from a lot of people.

Don't just rely on one person, no matter how smart they are. Have different mentors for different things. Find one for business, one for relationships, one for exercise, one for being a parent. Find a mentor for one side of your business, then another mentor for the other side of your business—see what I mean? You're already doing it. You found me, right? I'm mentoring you right now, within the pages of this book, so keep seeking guys like me out.

As you get older, you'll look back and realize that you've had mentors for certain stages of your life and then you moved on. And that's okay. You will never forget the people who helped you. I certainly haven't forgotten all the people who helped me. My life story has been full of mentors like Fred Gross, Dom Laganella, Joel Appel, and Lewis Katz, just to name a few. I'll tell you their stories as we go forward. They aren't famous, but to me they are legendary for the wisdom and encouragement they provided. Most of my mentors didn't even know they were my mentors; they just thought they were being my friends!

And when you make it big, find a mentor for dealing with success. I had Lewis Katz, a lawyer who went into business and got so wealthy he and a few of his partners owned part of the New Jersey Nets, the New Jersey Devils, and the New York Yankees. I mention Lew because he passed away two years ago in a plane crash and I miss him. I remember I went to Lew in 1995, after I first sold half of Wilmar, and asked him, "Lew, you've been wealthy for a long time. Will you help me understand how you deal with money and family?" Lew gave me some great advice. And he won't be the last mentor I have. You think I'm done learning new things? It never ends! So go find some mentors!

5: LOOK SUCCESSFUL, ACT SUCCESSFUL, AND YOU'LL BE SUCCESSFUL

Here's the thing, people want to do business with successful people. So guess what? You have to look and act like you belong in the room to win people's business. This goes back to what I said at the start of the chapter. You have to believe it before anyone else will. Some people call it "faking it until you make it," but you can't fake it. You have to put yourself in the mindset that you believe. It's all about having a positive attitude and making your intentions clear to the world. You may not be the most sharply dressed person in the world, but you have got to make an effort to do your best with what you have. I'm not saying you have to drive an expensive car, but you need to drive a clean and presentable car.

Look at the actors you see on the big screen. For most of them, their first and longest-lasting acting job was just . . . acting successful before they were. In the movie *La La Land,* Mia has to put on a brave face at auditions, then put on her best clothes and go out on the town with the little money she could scrounge up, trying to find a way to meet the difference-makers in Hollywood. Even when she was about ready to give up, she ultimately came back for one more reading, the one that made her a big star. Almost every Hollywood actor who is successful today has a real-life story like that. Their goal was the same as everyone in the business world: to land a big fish. People noticed Natalie Portman and John Wayne the way they eventually noticed Mia. No one would have bought what she was selling if she hadn't presented herself like a winner, even when she was on the verge of moving back into her parents' place in Boulder City.

My mom will tell you I wanted to be a millionaire by seven years old. It was always on my mind. So from day one of my business career I acted the part. I had no money but I dressed like a professional. I wore a suit, which was the thing to do back then. It wasn't anything fancy, but it was pressed and clean.

Bottom line is, if you're shooting for the moon, you better act like an astronaut.

6: SWEAT EVERYTHING

Remember the book *Don't Sweat the Small Stuff* that came out in the nineties? I read it and took it to heart when it came to my personal life. Who cares if your spouse doesn't put the cap on the toothpaste or if your kid keeps spilling milk at the dinner table? Life is too short to be that much of a stickler.

But let me tell you, I hate that book when it comes to doing business. You've got to sweat the big stuff, you've got to sweat the small stuff—you've got to sweat everything.

Especially when you are running your own company. Who else is going to quality-control every aspect of your operation if not you? Sure, it's great if you get so big that you can hire someone to oversee quality control, but even then, you're putting the livelihood of your company in the hands of one employee. One! And I've always believed that, if you want something done right, you have to do it yourself, or at least oversee those doing it to make sure they're doing it right. I know some people may call me a micromanager—fine, okay—but I prefer to think of myself as a "perfection technician" who is enthusiastic about making things the best they can be. I'm not Steve-Jobs obsessive, but I can see how Apple got to be so great. A big part of it was Jobs being all over everything, even the tiniest of details. Sure, I've mellowed as I've gotten older and wiser. I learned to delegate once I fully trusted people to do their jobs. But back when I was in your position just starting out? No way. I was all over everything like Steve Jobs—and you should be, too!

Here's a perfect example from later in my career. I once invested in a startup company that manufactured premade martinis in plastic martini glasses. They looked exactly like glass until you picked one up and realized it was plastic. Anyway, we sold a bunch of different martinis, but the cosmo was our number one seller. You know what I'm talking about—those drinks Sarah

Jessica Parker used to suck down on *Sex and the City?*

Well I thought it would be a great idea for a product—you could sell them in hotel room minibars, on planes, at backyard barbecues, and at live events, no bartender required—so my private equity firm helped fund the deal.

But when the cosmo-in-a-glass came out, it was red, not pink. And our apple martinis were dark green when they should have been pale green. That may seem like no big deal, but it killed the product. No one knew what they were. They didn't look like cosmos or apple martinis, so no one bothered. You see, I didn't sweat the small stuff and it bit me in the ass. My partners convinced me that the color didn't matter. Well guess what? It mattered! The business tanked and I lost money. Bottom line: if it doesn't work perfectly, throw it out and get it right. Because if you don't, one of your competitors will!

7: UNDERSTAND YOUR BUSINESS MARKET SIZE

You can imagine what it's like being in the private equity game. You hear a lot of new business ideas for potential investment or simply to give someone business advice. I've heard hundreds if not thousands in my lifetime, some great and others not so great. Nevertheless, I've found I keep saying the same thing to a ton of aspiring entrepreneurs: "You've got a good idea, but is it important enough to be a business? Even if you get 100 percent market share (which means everyone who could buy your product or service does), how big would this business be?" People get so emotional about their business idea that they don't think about if they can make a living doing it.

Here is how the conversation usually goes: someone comes to me with a business idea and says, "Hey, I want to build this."

And I go, "Great—how big is the market?"

And they say, "I don't know, but it's big."

I say, "Okay, I'll give you the benefit of the doubt. Out of every one hundred people in the United States—how many do you think would be interested in buying your product?"

And they say, "Maybe 1 out of 100?"

"Okay, that's not bad," I answer. "One percent will buy it,

so that means out of 350 million people in this country, you're targeting 3.5 million potential buyers. Now tell me, will they buy your product once a year? Once a month? Once in a lifetime?" Then I have them put a pencil to the manufacturing cost and overhead, and it turns out that even if they got 100 percent market share, they couldn't build a sustainable profit off this great idea. It's just not that important. Like the investors on *Shark Tank* like to say, "It's a good idea, but it's not really a business."

I don't want to crush an energetic entrepreneur's spirit, so if I think the idea is good I'll say, "That said, it doesn't mean this can't be a product line extension for a similar business, so keep the ideas coming!" I don't want to squash your spirit either, but you need to think long and hard about any idea you have before you risk your livelihood on it. Do your market research and find out what your ceiling is, before you invest in a cash cow that will never produce enough milk for you to live on.

8: SELL A PRODUCT THEY NEED, NOT ONE THEY WANT

There are wants and needs in life. We all need to buy shoes, but who needs to wear a thousand-dollar pair of Jimmy Choos? Nobody. People want to buy Jimmy Choos because they are luxury status symbols. So, are you producing a "want" or a "need?" It's vital that you know what you're selling. Really think about it before you go into business. If you're selling a want, ask yourself, how hard is it going to be to sell a want this year when the marketplace is flooded with tons of junk we don't need?

Your business will have a much better chance to succeed if you're offering a product or service that a certain percentage of the population must own. Because let me tell you, when your customer has to buy your product from someone, it's not a complex sale. I'm not saying you have to sell bottled water in the desert, but you need to be able to position yourself in a market where your product is needed, valued, and used again and again, with no chance of burnout simply because people get tired of playing with your toy.

I learned this lesson after I started my first company. We had moved away from the retail hardware business to selling directly to apartment-building owners. And it dawned on me, *these maintenance guys aren't browsing the aisles looking for something to catch their eye. They have to buy this stuff from somebody.* They needed our products to do their jobs. After I realized that, the sales got much easier. I came up with a foolproof way to sell to a "need" customer. First, I got their business by offering the best price around, and then I kept their business by providing the best customer service around. It was that simple.

Now my nephew Marc, he sells life insurance. To me, that's the hardest kind of sale. You don't have to have life insurance, right? Health insurance, sure—everyone needs to go to the doctor. But most people will tell you, "I don't make enough money while I'm living. Why should I pay for someone to benefit from my death on the off chance I die this month? It's a luxury I can't afford!" Sure, your spouse thinks it's a necessity, especially if you're into extreme sport vacations, but you're saying, "Don't worry, honey, I'll be fine." And if you happen to die in a horrible bungee jumping accident while on vacation in Mexico—you'll already be dead, so what will you care?

Now, I've sold "want" items too. I already mentioned premade martinis. Who needs those to survive? Nobody. You have to market, hustle, and work much harder to move units when they are "want" items. So I'm telling you, sell a "need" and not a "want," and your life will be much easier, trust me!

9: BE A SECOND-MOVER PIONEER

People always talk about "the first-mover advantage," right? I don't buy it. I'm not a pioneer. Never have been. I've never done anything first. What I've done is do it better. I've made a career out of being the second guy in the door. Do I have something against innovation? Heck no, I love it—but it's better to invest in something that has a proven track record. Let the pioneers do all the research. Let them do all the hard work, go through all the bugs, and figure out what works. Let them find out who's the customer and who isn't. You can sit back and watch how the first guys did it, then try to improve it.

Second movers are all over the place now; people are spending zillions of dollars on them in the tech world, especially fintech companies. Take one of my current investments, Crestar Loan Funds. In this business, we acquire consumer loans from marketplace lending platforms like Lending Club and Prosper Marketplace. Lending Club pioneered the business and Prosper was an early follower. Both companies spent millions of dollars on their technology.

Then I heard of this other marketplace lending company that was rising fast, so I paid it a visit. I asked them, "What did you spend to build your business?"

And they said, "A million bucks."

So I asked, "What did you spend on your technology?"

And they said, "Two hundred grand."

So I said, "Wow. How did you do it for so much less?"

They didn't hand over their code, but it was pretty easy to see what they did and how they did it. So we just copied it. We didn't plagiarize them, but we took their blueprint and made it better.

Since then, I've created LendingOne, a real estate marketplace lender. Take one guess about what I'm doing? Second-mover advantage, people.

Pioneers usually die of bug bites and dysentery.

10: WINGING IT IS NOT A STRATEGY

One of the most uninspiring sentences I've ever heard spoken around a conference table is "Don't worry, it'll work out." Really? How do you know? It's unbelievable. When your business partners tell you not to worry because "It'll work out"—it's not going to work out. You can't just sit back and wait for life to happen because when you do, unexpected stuff usually happens. You have to be smart. You have to be prepared. You have to go in with your guns loaded and a well-devised plan of attack.

I can't stress this enough. When starting your own business, "winging it" is not an option. Repeat after me: knowledge is power. Why do you think it's one of the most overused aphorisms out there? Because it's true!

If you are about to make a sales pitch to a customer and you ask your salesperson, "What's the plan?" and he or she says, "Oh, we'll wing it," you're in trouble. Anytime one of my guys said that, my stomach turned. It drove me nuts. I'd say, "We've got to know everything about this prospect. We've got to know everything about this company. Do your homework!"

The more you know about a customer, a product, a market, or even an employee, the greater advantage you have. And I'm not just talking about business and sales; I'm talking about everything you do in this world. You can't just wing it through life. You'll never end up where you want to be if you don't know where you're going.

11: USE YOUR TIME WISELY

It doesn't matter what business you're in or where you live on the planet, you usually only have about eight hours a day to connect with your stakeholders. Make the most of them! Remember when I talked about the "rolling university" I had set up for my employees at Wilmar? I did it because I wanted to help them maximize their "windshield time," the unproductive time in a day when they had to be in your car, on a bus, or standing in line somewhere.

As all my employees know, I think of "windshield time" in a broader context. When I say "make the most of it," I'm not just talking about listening to a self-help YouTube clip while you're behind the wheel. I'm talking about maximizing every single minute in a workday when the window of opportunity is open to do things like contact existing clients, meet with business partners, talk to suppliers, or sell your services to potential new clients. These are the really important things that must be addressed during business hours.

We have rules in civilized society. You can't set a meeting with your stakeholders for midnight or call them up at 2 a.m. to talk business—people have families and need to sleep. Sure, if you do business with other time zones you may have more than eight hours to work with, and that's great for you. Make hay while the sun shines.

I had 450 field salespeople working for me in 2001. It drove me nuts when I stopped into one of their offices and found them filling out an expense report in the middle of the afternoon. I'd say, "Really? Can't you do that after hours? You're missing opportunities here." The same thing went for managers who called a sales meeting at 10 a.m. on a Tuesday. I'm not saying they should have brought employees in on a Saturday, unless it's for a special occasion, but I'd tell them, "Can we have this meeting either earlier or later in the day so we aren't cutting into prime business hours?"

When it comes to doing what is free in life, I'm particularly passionate about this one. I'm not saying you should ban offsite lunches or keep your employees chained to their desks all day— I'm just saying, be smart about how you manage their time. Explain your rationale and they will get it.

I like to lead by example, I personally like to get up very early in the morning and handle all my "after hours" tasks like emailing and doing paperwork. I even use that space in my day as a creative time to think about marketing. It helps me think because the phone isn't ringing and I'm mentally fresh. I also know a lot of people who like to do their "after hours" stuff at night. It's all about whatever works for you.

In this world of 24/7 email (and texting) connectivity—most ambitious businesspeople have accepted (and even embraced) the fact that they're never truly off the clock. But don't take advantage of it—no one wants to be forced to respond to an important email after hours. Trust me, you don't want to be the guy who is bothering your stakeholders when they're doing things like sleeping or spending time with their family. They will not be as receptive to your message.

If it's so important, do it during business hours. It's all about time management. Life is short, the days are shorter, and we all need to sleep. The time you have to do business is finite. Don't waste it!

12: YOU CAN KID OTHERS, BUT DON'T KID YOURSELF

I'll end this chapter on this note. There are a lot of people that kid themselves to the point of self-delusion. A lot of us have to be "excessively optimistic" about certain issues to make it through life, and I get that. But when it comes to doing business, you need to be honest with yourself. Look at your idea and your target market and assess yourself objectively. Find mentors to help you assess the likelihood of your business meeting your goals.

I've met a lot of entrepreneurs who get emotionally attached to an idea and think it's better than it really is. I've met a lot of small business owners who have grand plans, and think they're capable of more than they really are.

Excuse my French, but I've met a lot of bullshitters in my life.

I recently had one guy who told me he was the world's greatest salesman and sales manager, so I hired him to run sales at my company LendingOne. The problem was, he didn't hold people accountable, so I called him into my office one day and said, "Look in the mirror. You clearly convinced me back when I hired you. But I want you to look in the mirror and tell me what you really see." I said, "You can kid others, but don't kid yourself."

I offer the same advice to you.

We all have to be performers to sell ourselves to the outside world, but don't bring that song-and-dance routine home and try to sell it to yourself. I totally get that entrepreneurs must believe in their hearts that they can slay the dragon (believing is one of my first lessons in this chapter) but be honest with yourself about your strengths and weaknesses. Don't delude yourself into thinking you can slay the dragon with a popgun, or that son of a gun will toast you.

Now, I will never ever tell you to stop dreaming. That's not what I do. I admire people like you who dare to achieve what many consider impossible. It takes a lot of guts to even try. But take some time to pump the brakes while you're driving Mach 3 with your hair on fire. Have a circle of friends who will help give you a reality check when you need one (and we all do sometimes). And as Theodore Roosevelt reportedly said, "Keep your eyes on the stars but your feet on the ground."

KEY TAKEAWAYS

- Believe in yourself—make it your daily mantra.
- Find a mentor—you can always learn something new.
- Always be on time. The early bird catches the worm.
- Treat everyone with kindness and respect, especially the "gatekeepers" to success.
- Return calls and texts in 24 hours or less—response builds customer loyalty.
- Sweat every detail.
- Dress for success, even if you're down on your luck.
- Know your target market and whether your product can succeed.
- Selling a necessary product is easier than selling a luxury.
- Don't reinvent the wheel—let someone else do that.
- Leave nothing to chance.

CHAPTER 3

DO YOU HAVE ENTREPRENEURIAL DNA? (HINT: IT DOESN'T MATTER)

The man who goes farthest is generally the one who is willing to do and dare. The sure-thing boat never gets far from shore.

—Dale Carnegie

EVER NOTICE WHEN successful businesspeople are asked how they did it, you'll hear a lot of them say, "I was born with the DNA to do it?" Yeah, well, that's a nice sound bite, but if you ask me, success has little to do with your genes. Who cares if you weren't "born" to run a business? You need great genes if you want to play center for the Los Angeles Lakers, but anyone can be a successful entrepreneur.

Anyone.

Really, it comes down to resolve. How many of you want it so bad it keeps you up at night—so bad that it aches in your soul? That's what I want to know—because the person who wants it the most is usually the one that gets it.

So, are you in it to win it? You better be. What does the writer Malcolm Gladwell say? You need ten thousand hours to become great at anything? That's about right. You have to live and breathe your business. You can't treat it like a hobby; you can't even treat it like a job. It has to be your entire life. It takes a lot of willpower to commit to something so fully that you "refuse to lose," but that's what it's going to take—not DNA!

Now, you may be saying to yourself, "Wait a minute, Bill, I was born with a head for business. I've got the genes!" If so, great for you! If it's in your lifeblood, you'll know it. I'm a living testament to the term "born to sell." I was the kid with a lemonade stand. I didn't play Cowboys and Indians; I liked to play "office." I was selling door-to-door cookies at four years old. It's debatable whether I stole the cookies from my mother or she gave them to me. Either way, it was a hundred percent profit! I guess it's in your DNA if you become a door-to-door salesman at four. I definitely was a natural.

A WILL TO WIN IS EVEN BETTER

But being born to sell will only get you so far. I was also preternaturally focused on making a name for myself. I had an iron will from a very early age, probably because I kind of always felt like an outsider who had something to prove.

I was born in Brooklyn, New York. If I'd been raised there, maybe I wouldn't have had anything to prove. But I wasn't. When I was four, my dad, Marty, was working for a small chain of fifty-six department stores called E.J. Korvette's. It was like the Target or Walmart of its time. Dad started working there as a stockboy after he got out of the army, and by 1962, he was a hardware department manager in one of the New York stores.

One day, he got a promotion to become the regional hardware department manager for all the stores from Pennsylvania to Virginia. The job was based in South Jersey, outside of Philadelphia, so we packed up and moved.

My parents bought us a house in South Jersey in a small town called Marlton that was next door to a larger, more affluent town, Cherry Hill. Our new home was on the border of both towns. My parents didn't consider which school district was better or what the demographics were—they just bought the house that cost less.

Turns out, Marlton was no Brooklyn or even Cherry Hill; it

was, for the most part, a plain old farm town. There were cows everywhere, apple orchards, and lots of open space. I had never seen anything like it! The subdivision we moved into was only the second one built in Marlton; the highway through town, Route 70, had literally just gotten paved. Other than farms and the two subdivisions, the only things in town were a two-mile strip of road that had a gas station, diner, nursery, and farm supply store.

That was it.

Needless to say, it was a big deal moving away from Brooklyn. Of the 650 students in my high school graduating class, there were four Jewish people. Four. Because of that, I kind of felt like an outsider, at least in the early years. I'm not throwing a pity party for myself, but I got beat up in grade school for being Jewish. That was a shock to me because in Brooklyn everybody was Jewish. My parents obviously knew there was anti-Semitism in the world; they just didn't realize it would rear its head and slap me around in our shiny, new neighborhood! But it happened.

I still wonder if my life would have turned out differently if we had stayed in Brooklyn or if Dad had moved us to Cherry Hill, because being an outsider in Marlton really affected my behavior. How so? I guess I've always felt like I had to work harder than everyone else to succeed. Looking back, our move to Marlton helped to make me an independent and ambitious person who knew how to fight for what I wanted. It wasn't always a joyride, but it toughened me up and made me stronger.

Do you ever wonder what became of the kids who pushed you around the elementary school playground? I do, and I tell you what—if I happened to run into any of my past tormenters, I wouldn't be bitter. I'd thank them. Those little tyrants helped to mold me into the man I am today.

13: DO WHATEVER IT TAKES TO SUCCEED

A year after we moved to Marlton, my dad got a big promotion to be a hardware buyer for the entire chain, but the position was back in the Manhattan offices of E.J. Korvette's. The only problem was, we were living in South Jersey now! Dad and Mom talked about it, and he said, "You know what? I'll commute. It's a great job. I'm going to meet opportunity halfway and do whatever it takes to succeed."

This was a big lesson to a junior businessman in training like me, and it should be for you, too. Opportunities in life don't always look like you think they will. They often come in different packages than you imagine. It may come in the form of a job halfway across the country or on another continent—or it may come as an opportunity to adapt your big idea to a different industry than you originally envisioned. You have to be flexible to optimize all the possibilities the world offers.

If you're ever given a business opportunity that seems out of your league, don't assume it can't be done. Fear is a poor advisor. Don't listen to what it has to say. Be smart. Be brave. And be prepared to meet the universe halfway when your name is called.

That's what my dad did—for fifteen years, he commuted two hours each way on a Trailways bus to and from New York. Every day.

FOR FIFTEEN YEARS

My First Product
So there I was, a chubby little Jewish kid living in this strange goyim town, a fish out of water in the throes of culture shock. What did I do? I found my passion and got interested in my first hobby, which (you guessed it) was making money! I knew I wanted to be rich, so I remember thinking, *Why should I sit around playing games? Why play with Monopoly money when I could be out there trying to make some real money? There's no better time than the present, right?*

So off I went, determined to make some dough. My parents probably thought I was nuts. I remember spending time in my R&D lab (my room) thinking of different products I could sell. I invented my first item when I was about eight years old. I started making pencil holders out of orange juice concentrate cans! I glued plywood to the cans that my Uncle Harold cut up for me, pasted Popsicle sticks on them, painted them, and went door-to-door selling them. I took custom orders: for an extra twenty cents, I'd put your Polaroid picture on it.

They didn't sell like hula hoops or hotcakes, but I made enough to put some money in my piggy bank. Getting out and meeting our neighbors was also a good exercise for me. You can tell I'm not exactly shy, but I taught myself to be outgoing by socializing myself through all my business ventures when I was a kid.

Soon everyone was my friend.

14: WHAT GOES AROUND COMES AROUND

Ever heard of the phrase "What goes around comes around?" It's so true, especially in the business world. The world may seem like this huge place when you're starting out, but just you wait. As you get older, it begins to shrink. You start to see people come back into your life that you thought you'd never see again.

You just never know when some person will reappear in your world and be in a position to help you—so don't burn bridges. Never let your emotions get the best of you if a business deal doesn't go your way. Always be professional. Don't be a hothead and blow off steam because you think, *Who cares? I'll never see those yahoos again.* You may regret it one day!

I remember being five years old, watching guys pour concrete for the sidewalk in front of our new house in Marlton. Later that day, some guy comes pulling up in his Cadillac, and what did he see? Me etching my initials into the wet cement! I remember the guy busted me: boy, did he yell. He walked me up to my front door and told my mom. I, of course, apologized.

It turns out that guy was the builder of the whole subdivision. His name was Tony Chiusano. Good thing I wasn't some teenager who told him to go suck an egg, because one day, many years later, I went into a meeting to try to win the business of an apartment building—and guess who owned it? Tony Chiusano. I introduced myself and told him about the wet cement vandalism story. Can you believe he remembered me marking his concrete? Anyway, he became a great customer.

I was only a kid when he caught me carving up his sidewalk, so I had no idea I'd ever see him again, but you're old enough to see the lesson here, right? What goes around comes around. Be nice to everybody! Be nice to the gatekeepers, be nice to the second in charge, and don't burn any bridge, because one day, you may need to cross it again. You'll be amazed how many times your universal diplomacy will pay off.

It's called building good karma.

15: KNOW WHEN A GOOD OPPORTUNITY FALLS IN YOUR LAP

This lesson may sound like it contradicts popular wisdom, but here's a little secret that many so-called experts will never admit: most of the best opportunities in life fall right out of the sky and into your lap. That's why they call them great opportunities! You usually don't have to go off on a wild goose chase to nab that elusive golden goose. Most of the time, it's as simple as some guy saying to you, "Hey, see that goose over there? What color is it?" Then boom, you gotta go grab that thing.

All of the best opportunities I ever had were just sitting there for anyone to take. If they hadn't fallen into my lap, they would have fallen into someone else's—so don't overlook the low-hanging fruit staring you in the face. Reach out and grab it! British business magnate Richard Branson says opportunities are like buses. If you miss one, there's always another one coming. I agree with him, but still—don't miss the one right in front of you. Life is too short. Another one may be coming, but you may be miserable waiting for it!

My earliest memory of taking advantage of a good opportunity that fell into my lap happened when I was in grade school. I loved going to New York with Dad to hang around his office when I had days off from school. Dad was good friends with this automotive buyer named Bernie. So, to give me something to do, Bernie started giving me massive amounts of automotive stickers for free with logos like STP and Valvoline on them. Sure, I liked stickers, but what the heck was I going to do with two hundred of them, wallpaper my room? I looked around the schoolyard and noticed a lot of the kids thought it was cool to put automotive stickers on their bikes. Voila, I had an idea. Take one guess what I did next.

Stickers became my next item, and did those babies sell! They sold so well, I ran out of the ones Bernie gave me, so I wrote letters to every oil and car manufacturing company to see if they would send me stickers, and some did.

I remember I'd made thirty-six bucks off my sticker empire by April 10, 1971, which happened to be the day my baby sister Lisa was born. I only remember this fact because my older sister Amy and I stayed at a friend's house when my parents were at the hospital. Guess what? Our house was robbed, and my $36 was stolen! It may sound a little nuts, but it still makes me cry today.

16: TURN YOUR PASSION INTO YOUR TRADE

I know of one recipe for happiness that works for pretty much everyone who can find a way to do it. If you can make your passion your business, you will have a fulfilling career and always love what you do. The happiest people I know do what they love. They live to work in the best possible way. Look at Roger Ebert. He lived and breathed movies—he would never dream of doing anything else for a living. He woke up every morning and was excited to go to work. He would have written about movies even if no one paid him. That's called having a passion for your business.

So think about your life: you've got this big idea, right? Are you in love with it? I hope it's something you'd be ecstatic to eat, sleep, and breathe every day for years. It has to pump you up just thinking about doing it for a living. It definitely helps if it's something you enjoy in your spare time.

You might be saying: "But Bill, does this mean selling hardware is your passion?" Hey, just because it's not your hobby doesn't mean you can't love doing it. That was just one part of my career, but let me tell you, when I was running Wilmar, I was a plumbing savant! I was a hardware geek who loved to talk shop with the maintenance guys. I knew every nut and bolt—every piece of hardware we sold was because I truly was passionate and loved doing it.

That said, I'm passionate about a lot of things, and always have been. I'm always looking to turn my passions into a business in some way, shape, or form.

Here are two examples from the opposite ends of my career. The first one happened when I was fourteen and had a passion for photography; I was a shutterbug. I had a Minolta SRT 101 35mm camera and took pictures of everything under the sun. I even had a darkroom in my basement.

I liked to hang out at this camera store that was across the highway from my house. I'd tell my mom, "I'm gonna run across the highway to the camera store," and she'd say, "Okay, bye!" No one was afraid I'd get run over by an eighteen-wheeler! It was a different time.

I got friendly with the owners of the store, and one day, they said, "You know, Billy, we like you. Do you want to work behind the register and sell film to customers?"

I said, "Great," and started working there. Why not? I got a free education on how to be a professional photographer. I was too young to be put on the payroll, so they paid me in film and photo paper, which was perfect because my parents couldn't pay for this hobby; it was too expensive.

So one day, I was working behind the register and thinking about how I could take my passion to the next level. I got an idea: I would start a business called Bill Green Photography, which turned out to be my first business card. I took pictures of little kids and dogs. I even traded work at the camera store to buy professional lighting equipment, even though I didn't have a studio. Instead, I took my business on the road and into people's homes. I never could figure out how to get the shadows out of my photos, but the people loved them anyway.

This led me to selling photos at school. I wasn't an athlete, but I was friends with everybody, so I'd go to the high school basketball and football games and take action shots of the athletes. After the game, I'd go home to develop the film and print contact sheets. The next day, I'd take them to school and sell black-and-white photos to the athletes. I knew who the guys with big egos were, who the rich kids were, and who could afford them—so I knew my target market. I had five or six customers on each team, and that's what I did throughout high school.

Fast-forward forty years later, and here I am, starting LendingOne at fifty-seven years old. I'm truly passionate about this business and am putting my heart and soul into making it a huge success. But my mind never stops thinking about merging passion with business—I can't help it. It's what I do! So I look at my life today. What are my hobbies?

I've been competing in local triathlons for the past twenty-seven years, and I've been collecting fine wines for twenty. I know triathlons will never be my business, so one day, I was talking to a good friend, and he said, "Bill, if you're going to do anything else, you've got to do what you love and fulfill a passion. I think you would love being in the wine business."

I said, "You know, you're spot on."

So I'm thinking about finding a way to make wine a part of my business. Why? Because it's a recipe for happiness. I went on a tear trying to figure out how to get into the game. I realized there was no way I could open a winery in Napa. If the restaurant business is risky, the winery business is very risky, and so ego-driven that only movie stars and super rich guys are buying winery up.

There's this old joke: Do you know how to have a million-dollar winery? Start with two million!

I began looking at a few unconventional ways to get in the business. I thought outside of the box. I looked at companies that made corks. I looked at companies that made barrels. I looked at all kinds of different things surrounding the wine business. I even contemplated opening a wine storage facility. I'm still thinking about how to get involved. I will never give up. In fact, by the time you read this book, I may have figured it out! I haven't decided what I will name my winery, so check back for updates!

If you're looking for a way to jump into an area you're passionate about with all your heart, you have to throw a relentless amount of unconventional thinking into it. Don't give up. Think of a way to get involved—somehow!

THE REST OF MY CHILDHOOD CAREER

Besides my photography career, the rest of my childhood jobs were all over the map—as you shall see. Some kids built tree houses and went to summer camp. I went to summer camp, all right, but I scrubbed toilets and flipped burgers for the other campers!

Once I started working, I never stopped.

Probably my first "real" job was in the newspaper business. It wasn't like I had a lot of options when I was twelve! Back then, at least in New Jersey, kids couldn't get a real job until they were fifteen. The only way you could legally work for a company as a minor was to become a newspaper delivery boy, so I did.

But I didn't just become an average paperboy. I took it to the next level.

There were two parts to being a newspaper boy. One was riding around the neighborhood on your bicycle and throwing newspapers on the doorsteps of subscribers. The other was going door-to-door collecting money every other week.

My subdivision had six hundred homes, and we had three main papers: the *Philadelphia Inquirer*, the *Philadelphia Bulletin*, and the South Jersey *Courier-Post*. I ended up working for the *Inquirer* and *Bulletin* first. I delivered the *Inquirer* in the morning and the *Bulletin* in the afternoon, seven days a week.

I was busting my hump—hustling all over the neighborhood, delivering, and collecting. I had to hit a ton of houses a day because it was rare that one home got multiple papers, but it was cool when it happened.

I was doing pretty well working for those two papers—but one day I got to looking at the *Courier-Post* and thought, *I'd love to corner the neighborhood market and deliver for them too. But I'm only one kid. I only have two arms and two wheels!*

So I got creative.

I couldn't add even more newspapers to my bicycle, or I would fall over from all the weight—so instead I became a "paper station" for the *Courier-Post*. That meant a van from the *Courier-Post* came by my house every afternoon and dropped off two hundred or so newspapers. It was my job to sort the papers into stacks for the individual neighborhood paperboys to pick up.

I'd get up before sunrise every morning and deliver my *Inquirers*. When I got home from school, I sorted the *Courier-Post* papers in my garage.

I'd say, "Okay, paperboy Joey, you get twenty-five papers, and paperboy Tony, he gets thirty," and so on. Joey and Tony would come by and pick up their stacks at my house. Then I'd hop on my bike and deliver my *Bulletins* around the neighborhood.

Needless to say, I didn't get a lot of sleep as a child. I was a busy kid! But I still found time to have fun. I'm a big basketball fan, so I played a lot of basketball with my friends, and I also founded the Marlton chapter of the Philadelphia 76ers Fan Club—of which I was president, of course!

There I was. My newspaper empire was going great, but I was burning out. I was a twelve-year-old with three different jobs while also going to school full-time. It started to get overwhelming. Newspapers were invading my subconscious. I was dreaming of newspapers!

I learned how to delegate for the first time in my career. I met this neighborhood kid named Stevie Garzinski who agreed to separate the *Courier-Post* papers for me. He was my first employee. The *Courier-Post* paid me two bucks a day, so I cut Stevie in by paying him a dollar a day. I had officially become a newspaper distribution tycoon in training!

But then I got older and realized I could be more than that. I took other jobs. I worked at summer camps when I was fifteen. When I was sixteen, I worked at Dairy Queen, but I could never get my double (or triple) swirl cones to stand up straight, so they fired me! I got a job as a porter at Dunkin' Donuts and then flipped burgers at Bob's Big Boy. When I was seventeen, I sold cleaning chemicals for Bestline Products door-to-door. I remember one time this lady (who knew me from my paper route) invited me into her home to do a demonstration. It didn't go well.

"Look, your stain is gone!" I said, proudly pointing to her clean carpet.

"What about that big white spot you left in its place?" the lady replied.

Good thing she was nice: she didn't get mad or sue me.

After that fiasco, I decided to focus on selling Bestline's most popular product, Zif, an all-purpose cleaner. I sold to places like retail stores and gas stations. This was my first commercial sales job.

17: EMBRACE THE AHA MOMENT

Then came New Year's Eve 1976—a day that changed my life forever. It was my seventeenth birthday, and I finally got my driver's license. I was riding high and ready for action, so the next thing I needed was a date. Lucky for me, I had one—a blind date, no less, for New Year's Eve.

Her name was Andrea, and we really hit it off. I took her out in this pretty cool Dodge Charger that I shared with my older sister, Amy, who coincidentally had just started dating Andrea's brother, Steve, at the time.

It was perfect. We were one big happy family. My relationship with Andrea led to the first big "aha" moment of my young life.

You see, one day, I was talking to Steve, and he said, "What do you think about selling T-shirts at flea markets?"

I said, "Okay, what's a flea market?"

Steve explained it to me, and I thought about it, then asked my dad for his opinion.

Dad said, "Why would you want to do that? There's going to be a ton of people selling T-shirts at the flea market. Why don't you sell something different?"

I said, "Okay, like what?"

He said, "I have a lot of samples in my office that vendors send me that never get put on the shelf. I'll send them to you."

A few days later, a giant carton wound up on my front door, full of hardware items like hammers, pliers, and all kinds of tools. I opened it up, and my eyes got as big as saucers. I remember thinking, *We can work with this.* I had no idea what some of it was, but it looked like stuff somebody out there needed to get a job done. Even then, I knew it was better to sell a need item than a want item like T-shirts, which everyone and their dog was selling.

There I was, armed with all this loot. Steve and I jumped in the car, drove out to the Berlin Flea Market, and set up a table. Remember, we didn't pay for any of our inventory, so just like the cookies and the stickers, it was 100 percent profit. Plus, it was all brand-new hardware, so when a customer asked me how much, I'd say "Okay, this hammer's a dollar, and that wrench is fifty cents."

I didn't know it at the time, but I was offering a great price for all this brand-new hardware. Of course, it didn't take me long to figure it out once I saw people were going crazy for it! We were selling out every time we went to a flea market. I remember tallying our earnings at the end of one day, looking up at Steve, and saying, "I think we're onto something here."

We sure were, and it was all because I embraced the aha moment. And it was so easy. I had taken both Steve and Dad's ideas—and boom, it was magic time!

18: MAKE LEMONADE OUT OF THE LEMONS LIFE DEALS YOU

Our flea market business was going so well, we started running out of product. Dad only had so many free samples to send us, so I started scavenging the neighborhood looking for anything we could sell. I did whatever it took; I even started picking through trash in the rich Cherry Hill neighborhoods. I'd drive around saying, "I think I could sell that." Then I'd throw it in the back of the car.

I loved the hoarders. Anytime I'd meet one, I'd offer my services.

"Hi, ma'am. Can I help you clean out your garage, for no charge?"

Those little old ladies thought I was a saint.

Then bad luck and serendipity struck at the same time.

A few months had passed, and Andrea and I had broken up. Meanwhile, Amy and Steve had also broken up. Steve wasn't interested in flea markets anymore, but I still had the business going and wanted to keep doing them.

I remember the day my dad lost his job, after working at E.J. Korvette's for twenty-eight years. He came home and sat us all down around the kitchen table. He said his company was going through something called "corporate downsizing" and they had to lay off some of their more experienced employees, which made no sense to me. Why would any company lay off their best employees? I was one baffled kid, but Dad seemed to take it all in stride.

Later that night, he came into my bedroom and said, "Look, Billy. While I'm out of work, I'm going to help you out at the flea market."

He had connections in the industry thanks to his time as a buyer at E.J. Korvette's. I'll give it to Marty, he had established a lot of great relationships with people who owned or worked at major hardware companies, so we didn't have to rely on scavenging anymore.

He and I would go to their offices in New York or visit their factories, and they would sell us hardware for great prices. So there I was, suddenly buying hardware at prices that only the large retailers could—it was great.

It didn't take long for me to realize my dad was a better partner than Steve!

MY FIRST MENTOR PAYS OFF

Then I found my first mentor. I wasn't looking for one, but one day, Dad introduced me to a man named Fred Gross. Fred was a Cherry Hill guy whose family owned a plumbing company called Hancock Gross. Fred and I really hit it off. He was their vice president of sales, and I learned a lot about sales and business from him.

I remember thinking Hancock Gross had an interesting business model. They sold plumbing items to retailers, but didn't make anything themselves; they were packagers who imported everything. So Fred and I would talk shop a lot. He was a charismatic person with a super personality. Granted, he was a "plumbing guy," but hey, I thought that was cool! I'd listen to Fred talk about how they developed their product lines and took them to market. This may sound like boring stuff, but it wasn't to me: I was enamored of his family business. When most boys my age wanted to be Burt Reynolds or Reggie Jackson when they grew up, I wanted to be Fred Gross.

Fred saw how enthused I was about my own business, so he started to invite me down to visit his distribution center in Philadelphia, where Hancock Gross had this space called the Retail Buy Back room. This room was heaven to a guy like me.

Inside it was tons of plumbing items Hancock Gross couldn't sell at retail. Why? They were "returned items" by new customers or products from former suppliers. So Hancock Gross had to unload this stuff, since it would cost too much to repackage. Say an item had an original retail price of one dollar, Fred would sell it to me for 50 percent and then give me 50 percent off that, which meant I could buy it for a quarter and then charge 50 cents to our flea market customers. Fred let Dad and me scrounge around and pick anything we wanted to take to the flea market. It beat garbage can diving!

This was a huge step for us. Fred really helped us evolve our business. Think about it: our value proposition was our great pricing, right? That's why our customers loved us, but with access to the Hancock Gross Retail Buy Back Room, we now had great margins too, which meant we had the power to be a great discounter while being very profitable.

That's what I call a winning combination.

19: YOU CAN DO GREAT THINGS WHEN FAILURE IS NOT AN OPTION

I was working flea markets six days a week. Florence, my mom, was as well. Even my older sister Amy was working with us. It was a real family affair. I'm telling you, my parents were two of the hardest-working people I've ever known.

I was still a senior in high school, so I was in a program that allowed me to get out of school at noon to work. I hired some of my friends to work for us. Soon, we had the manpower to work five or six flea markets at once.

We were a well-oiled flea market machine!

This was when I realized you can do anything once you know it has to be done. Sometimes, that means playing psychological tricks on yourself to will yourself to success. Other times, you really have to succeed, or your entire family will go in the tank. That's what the flea market business was to me. My dad never got another job at a department store for the rest of his life. He was all in. This business I had started had become our family business. It was the only thing putting food on our table.

I don't know if you're in a similar position, but having your entire family count on you is quite a motivating factor. Know what I mean? I'm sure a lot of you do.

I needed to succeed, so I did what I had to do.

I dug through trash. I got my hands dirty. I even slept in cars to get business! There was a flea market called Englishtown that I wanted to work—but the only problem was we didn't have a reserved spot. What did I do? I loaded up the trunk of my parents' Oldsmobile with our goods the night before and slept in the backseat so I could get a spot. You see? I wanted it more than the next guy. I was going to get that spot. But that's what you have to do to win. And we had to win.

Failure was no longer an option.

20: CREATE MULTIPLE PROFIT ARMS FOR YOUR BUSINESS

By this time, we had expanded our offerings, and were selling plumbing supplies, hardware, glassware, auto seat covers, and frying pans all over New Jersey and Philadelphia. Our T-FAL no-stick frying pans were now our number-one item. Go figure. People couldn't get enough of them because, at the time, they were the only no-stick kind on the market. To buy one at a retail store was very expensive, so people loved getting them for a discount.

It all started because my mom met a guy at the Columbus Flea Market who got all the irregular T-FAL frying pans from their national distribution center in New Jersey. Mom, she knew quality kitchenware when she saw it.

She said, "Billy, this is a great product. Let's make a deal with this guy."

So we started buying frying pans in massive quantities. A pan that was eighteen to twenty bucks in the store, he sold to us for three bucks. We sold them for six.

We were doing so well, our garage back home couldn't hold our inventory. One day, I came home to find every square inch of our house was loaded with cartons. It looked like we'd become a family of hoarders ourselves. Our living room was floor-to-ceiling cartons. Our dining room was stuffed to the gills, with boxes all over the place.

Finally, Mom put her foot down and said, "This is crazy. We have got to get these out of here!"

Dad said, "Okay, you're right. Billy, let's look for a hardware store."

I thought, *Great idea*. The idea with the hardware store was not only to create another profit arm, which is a great idea for any business—but if we could just make enough money from sales to pay rent and our expenses, the hardware store would be a free storage facility for our flea market inventory. *Pretty smart*, I thought.

MICHAEL'S HARDWARE IS BORN

After looking around, we found the perfect place right outside of Camden—Michael's Hardware. It was a mom-and-pop that had just closed. There was no inventory, but it had shelves, an old cash register, and all the equipment we needed—so it was move-in ready.

We made the move.

On April 1, 1977, we moved into the store and took its brand name. Before that, we had just called it "the business," but now we were official. Now we were Michael's Hardware. We talked it over and decided to make our business official too. I put in $2,000 and owned a third of the business, and Mom and Dad put in $4,000 and owned two-thirds of it. My grandparents also loaned us $10,000, so with $16,000 we officially launched Michael's Hardware, which eventually became Wilmar.

We didn't realize it at the time, but looking back, it was a monumental moment in all our lives. But now we had to stock our store! If you want people to come to your hardware store, you have to have a little bit of everything, so we used the ten grand my grandparents had loaned us to buy inventory.

Of course, Dad, being the connected guy he was, knew how to get all the hardware store supplies. He knew this wholesale distributor down the street called Nu Way Distributors where we could buy everything. They had items Hancock Gross didn't have—but the only catch was, you had to be a hardware store to buy from them, which we now were! Boom, we stocked up and opened our doors.

We were still technically a flea market retailer, but we legitimized our business when we opened Michael's Hardware.

And that is how it all got started.

IT TAKES ALL YOU HAVE

I just gave you a tried-and-true blueprint for turning your own startup into a successful small business. Times have changed, but the lessons stay the same. I hope you realize how much effort my family and I put into getting my first business off the ground.

It was not a hobby. It was not a job. It was our lives.

We lived and breathed it 365 days a year. We worked hard every day and then came home and worked some more. When we ate dinner together, we talked shop, nonstop. We weren't watching television or talking about normal family stuff (whatever that is!), because we all had a passion for what we were doing—and failure was not an option.

If you only take one thing away from this chapter, I want you to work on developing an iron will and an unbending intent for making your big idea a reality, because you'll need it to achieve your dream.

Once you realize that failure is not an option and there is no fallback plan, then the whole world will open up for you.

I will end with this: if I ever get an opportunity to talk with you about being a potential investor in your business, and I see that you are packing a great idea and you have those two invaluable traits of iron will and unbending intent in your tool set—I will tell you not to listen to the nonbelievers and that you can do anything in this world.

DNA be damned.

KEY TAKEAWAYS

- You may be born to sell, but a will to succeed is even better.
- What goes around, comes around—you never know when the wheel of fortune is going to turn for or against you. Be prepared for either outcome.
- Don't let adversity keep you down—harness that energy to fuel your passion.

- Be willing to do whatever it takes to optimize your potential.
- Recognize a great idea when it appears.
- If you have an idea, act on it; there's no time like the present.
- Don't burn bridges—you never know who or what may come back to help you in the future.

CHAPTER 4

BOOTSTRAPPING A STARTUP

*I'm a great believer in luck. And I find
the harder I work, the more I have of it.*

—Thomas Jefferson

I WAS A big a fan of comic books growing up, so I get the current obsession with superheroes in movies and on TV: they're everywhere. One thing that hasn't changed in all these years is that every superhero has a great origin story, right? You know, Superman came from Krypton, Spider-Man got bitten by a radioactive spider, Batman trained himself to be the ultimate crimefighter—well, now you know my business's origin story. We may not have looked like we had any superpowers yet, but our little hardware store was about to turn into a big, swinging behemoth in the industrial supply market.

And we weren't going to wait to luck into powers like Superman or Spider-Man did. We'd have to develop them ourselves.

So how did we go from Bruce Wayne to Batman?

First, I maintained a healthy mindset even after we started to make some money. I had a clear vision and knew exactly where I wanted to go. I never looked to grow sideways; I was always looking to grow up.

I had my eyes on the prize.

I thought big and acted big to be big. Every smart entrepreneur should take this one to heart, but don't get too full of yourself. You have to be smart. No matter what kind of business you're starting—from a tech company to a high-end cupcake company—it's crucial that you have a healthy vision for the future of your company. What does that mean, exactly?

A healthy vision is one that is not so inflated that it's fueled by delusional thinking, but it's also not so small that you're limiting yourself.

What's that old saying? "There's a thin line between love and hate?" Well, there's a thin line between thinking too big and thinking too small. You have to thread that needle. To do that, you want to aim high but stay grounded. Believe in yourself, but talk to mentors. Have confidants who will shoot straight with you! And whatever you do, don't drive blind, because we all know where a wing-and-a-prayer strategy will get you in the business world . . . into bankruptcy court.

Accept the fact that you are going to make a few mistakes (even the best do), but learn from them. Get back up on the horse, and keep riding. If you stay flexible and creative—and keep adapting with the times (while working your butt off)—you'll get to the Promised Land.

Believe it.

I hope my company's origin story inspired you. It should! When it comes to starting from nothing, you can't get much smaller than us. Our business came to life out of one carton of free hardware supplies. How much smaller can you get? Think of it this way: if I could do it, how hard can it be for you to do it too?

DO BATTLE WITH COMPLACENCY EVERY DAY

Let's shift gears and presume you're at the same point in your business that I was back in 1978—you're off and running. Are you jacked up to grow your business organically? You are? Awesome, that's what Coach Green wants to hear!

Harness that enthusiasm, and use it wisely because you don't want to get fat on your success. A lot of entrepreneurs can fall into the trap of getting complacent once they reach their initial goals. Why? I have no idea. It's almost like some of them don't have enough dreams in their head to keep coming up with more.

That was never my problem!

Never get too satisfied by your success. When you hit a milestone—great, go have a steak dinner. Pop a cork, if you must—but you expected to be here, right? So get back to the office, and don't waste time doing a touchdown dance. That's what true winners do. They act like they've been in the end zone before.

Set another goal for yourself. Hell, set five more goals. Keep reaching for the next rung in the ladder—and dare to be the best you can be. One of your big goals should be to get so good at what you do that the big players in your industry can no longer ignore you. That's what I was doing at this point in my career. And let me tell you—did it work.

SOMETHING IN THAT NEW JERSEY WATER

I had no clue that one table at a flea market would turn into a billion-dollar business, but I also never thought it wouldn't happen, either. If I wanted a role model, all I had to do was look around my hometown to find an entrepreneur who wildly exceeded all expectations.

Can you believe there was another amazing startup going on in Marlton right around the same time we were? There must have been something in the water, and I don't mean toxic waste.

You see, back in 1973, a little bank called Commerce Bank was founded just a quarter-mile from my home on Route 70. It grew and grew from a small bank to become one of the largest banks on the East Coast, with more than four hundred branches. It was founded by a guy named Vernon Hill, who revolutionized the banking industry by providing amazing customer service never seen before in the retail banking world. It was unprecedented. He wrote a great book I highly recommend to you, *Fans Not*

Customers: How to Create Growth Companies in a No Growth World.

Hill was definitely a different kind of banker. He still is! He was a former fast-food restaurant guy who transformed the traditional banking blueprint by operating more like a retailer. He bent over backwards to please his customers. He cared so much about the client experience that he built his entire business model around it.

After he sold Commerce Bank to TD Bank, Hill started Metro Bank in London with the same business model, and it's doing great. That's a pretty big deal. Did you know there hadn't been a new bank startup in London in a hundred years?

Anyway, seeing what he was doing right up the street was inspirational. It felt great to know I wasn't the only entrepreneur in Marlton thinking big. He kept me aiming high!

ADAPT, ADAPT, ADAPT!

Back in 1978, Michael's Hardware and our flea market business had a pretty good thing going, but I wasn't satisfied. I knew I wanted to keep growing.

Then, guess what? My want became a need.

We hit an iceberg that threatened to sink our ship. This happens in business, so don't be surprised when it happens to you, too. I'm not a big science guy, but it's actually a law of physics. Have you ever heard the phrase "From order comes chaos?" Well, it's true in the universe, in life, and in the business world. Plan for it. You're always going to be putting out fires, so be prepared to change course at a moment's notice.

This time, we had a fire drill that forced us to adapt our business model once again—we lost our number one flea market item, T-FAL frying pans. We were a victim of our own success. We were moving so many "irregular" frying pans that people were taking them into department stores and saying, "Hey, I bought this frying pan from you, and look, it's scratched. I want a new one," cheating the department stores. So our supplier got cut off!

We were devastated, but we immediately started thinking

about how to replace that income. I looked at Dad and said, "This means now the hardware store has to make money."

It was no longer just a luxury, no longer just a glorified storage space for our flea market goods. Now it was time for the hardware store to step up and start making a real profit. But how? There were hardware stores all over the place. What could we do to stand out?

SELLING TO COMMERCIAL CLIENTS

We had to get creative, so we started brainstorming about how we could differentiate ourselves in the marketplace. One day, Dad mentioned that back in Brooklyn, his uncle used to own a hardware store that offered charge accounts to the local apartment complex owners. It was good business for him.

"Let's look into that," I said. "Think any local complex owners would be interested?" The moment those words came out of my mouth, I looked out the window of our hardware store and noticed there were several apartment complexes right across the street!

Dad said, "Go pick up some preprinted credit applications from the office supply store. Then I want you to put on a suit and visit all the apartment complex owners in the area. Give them our credit application. Tell them we're here if they need anything."

This was our new plan.

It sounded like a pretty smart thing to do, especially when we were trying to keep our business from sinking into the Atlantic! We were adapting to the changing times while looking to grow, not because we wanted to.

Now we had to.

So after school, I put on my best (and only) suit and started pounding the pavement. I remember the first place I visited. The manager of the complex said, "We don't buy from hardware stores, kid."

I said, "Who do you buy your hardware from?"

He said, "We buy from this company, and they deliver. Here's their catalogue."

I said, "Hmm, a catalogue." I took the catalogue and filed that idea away.

I visited every apartment complex in our area. Then, one day, I got a call from one of the apartment complex managers I'd met. Their maintenance manager wanted to order three paintbrushes. Not a big sale, but the big deal was that we gave him the order on a credit account and delivered it the same day.

That was our first commercial sale.

I knew in my gut this was a big untapped market in our area. I could feel the opportunity knocking, but I had to do my homework to be sure. I wanted to know as much as I could about these new potential customers. I hit the streets again and widened my net; I started meeting and greeting as many apartment complex owners, managers, and maintenance managers as I could.

I asked one of them if I could check out his maintenance shop. He said, "Sure, why not? Let me show you where we buy our stuff." So he took me back to his shop where his maintenance manager for his two hundred apartment units kept his supplies. The guy showed me everything. He said, "We buy all this stuff from this company and all that stuff from that company—and for our plumbing supplies, we buy from this company called Pier Angeli. Here's their catalogue."

Another catalogue, I thought.

That night, I went back to the hardware store and talked to Dad.

I said. "These guys don't buy from hardware stores; they buy from companies that have catalogues and salespeople. We need a catalogue."

Dad asked, "How are we going to do that? We're a hardware store."

"Leave that to me," I said.

MY MARKETING OBSESSION
PAYS OFF

I retreated to the back office with my head full of ideas. For the first time, my brain started working on the marketing side of business. I'd never given it much thought until now—but seeing those catalogues had sparked something in my imagination.

I met with Fred Gross and asked him if he would let me use a Hancock Gross catalogue and put my own cover on it.

He said, "Sure, no problem."

Now we had our own catalogue. I used parts of the Hancock Gross catalogue for certain items and lifted pages from the Pier Angeli catalogue for the plumbing inventory Hancock Gross didn't sell.

Well, guess what happened next? It didn't take long before Pier Angeli sued me, so I had to stop! Remember, I was nineteen and had no idea what copyright infringement was—so of course the "cease and desist" order I received from Pier Angeli came as a total shock.

Once I realized I was breaking the law, I tossed those catalogues and started creating my own from scratch. I did it all by hand, with no computers. I'd cut out each individual picture of our products and paste them with a hot glue machine on paper. I had a Selectric typewriter to set what I'd type, and then I'd cut out the text with my utility knife. I had to press one letter at a time onto the page. This was the original cut-and-paste method! It was a lot of work, but I loved it.

I became obsessed.

Whenever I had any free time, I'd be in the back office working on the catalogue. Can you believe everybody laughed at me when they saw what I was doing?

Dad would come into my office and say, "Look, Billy's playing with his paper dolls again."

Everyone at the hardware store thought making a catalogue was a crazy thing to do—a waste of time. I didn't care. I knew this was the next logical step for us to build a larger client base. I created an eight-page monthly flyer that became a full catalogue. They were as primitive as could be, but they launched our business to a different level. We attracted a lot of price-sensitive customers who were tired of paying higher prices to bigger companies like Pier Angeli, which didn't deliver great customer service or offer one-stop shopping.

And it didn't take a rocket scientist to see the potential for a one-stop-shop business model. When I found out that plumbing supplies were only half of the budget for your average apartment building maintenance department, I knew companies like Pier Angeli were leaving a lot of revenue on the table. I mean, where were those guys getting the other half of their stuff? Eventually, they would be getting all their supplies from us—through our catalogue.

You better believe all the guys at the hardware store stopped laughing once they saw how successful our catalogues were! They became our hallmark. They made us unique. Catalogues are still a key part of the company's marketing strategy, even today. I knew I had scored one for the home team by believing in my vision when no one else did. But I didn't do a touchdown dance and shout, "In your face!" to anybody. Instead, I kept my head down and acted like I'd been there before. I got back to work. That's what champions do . . .

They keep their eye on the prize.

WILMAR IS BORN

So there we were. Business was rolling. We had survived another fire drill and come out of the flames even stronger. On January 1, 1979, we decided to change our name from Michael's Hardware to Wilmar Supply Company (Wil- for me, William, and -mar for my dad, Marty). We had stopped working the flea markets, but still had the hardware store. The big difference was we were now selling almost exclusively to apartment building owners and their maintenance departments on credit accounts through our catalogues and field salespeople.

Our spreadsheet looked better than my report card ever had! In 1977, which was a partial year for us, the business sales were $75,000. In 1978, they were $300,000. In 1979, we did one million dollars in sales!

That's a lot of organic growth for two-and-a-half years. How did we do it? It wasn't by offering the lowest prices, that's for sure.

21: DON'T JUST BE THE LOW-COST PROVIDER

I talk to a lot of people with big dreams, and I've noticed a bunch of them seem to think if they offer a great product at the lowest price, then boom, that's all they need to do. I disagree. Most people will be attracted by price, but you can't hang your hat on price alone. You just can't sustain growth that way.

You have to offer more.

Sure, we stood out because we were the low-cost provider, and that got us up and running. But we paired our great price with amazing customer service. My motto was, "Get them on price. Keep them on service."

It doesn't matter what industry you're in. You can't be the lowest-cost provider and think you have a great business. Why? There's no way to differentiate yourself in the marketplace. There will always be someone who will do it for less—and whoever's the lowest bidder is always going to be the winner. Take Amazon; they got everybody on price, right? But they keep customers for being so damn convenient.

That's what we did. So don't put all your eggs in the discount basket, because that thing is full of holes. You've got to create a unique offering that only you can provide.

22: CREATE A NICHE. BE UNIQUE.

Before we entered the commercial market, the apartment supply industry was made up of product-line-specific vendors. Wilmar was the first one-stop-shop supplier in our area; it was a value prop our customers had never seen.

We would have never gotten to this point if we hadn't kept adapting our business model (from discount sales to retail sales to commercial sales) until we had created a unique niche for ourselves in the marketplace.

It's not just what you should do—it's what you must do if you want to remain successful in any line of business. Think about it: if we had stayed stuck in our old ways in any of our past incarnations, we would have sunk like the *Titanic* careening into a New Jersey iceberg.

But we didn't let the ship sink.

We built a better boat and kept striving and adapting until we became irreplaceable to our clients. This was why clients started buying from us instead of the larger companies like Pier Angeli.

When you bought from the big companies, you had to call in and wait for a salesperson to take your order, and then they would ship the stuff in a few days. We topped that by delivering everything the next day in our market. And we sold everything. Our customers would say, "I want six of these, four of these, some new keys, and a piece of glass, 18 x 24 inches." Back in 1979, nobody sold all those products in a catalogue, and that was pretty darn unique.

I know for a lot of businesses it's not possible, but if you are in the position to corner the market—do it. People these days love one-stop shopping. Again, just look at Amazon. I've been trying to corner the market ever since I had my paper route! It's a great way to build customer loyalty and eliminate the need for your customers to go to your competition to buy the other stuff that you don't have.

23: KNOW YOUR BUSINESS INSIDE AND OUT: BE A SAVANT

Now, let's fast-forward a couple of years to 1982. At this point, Wilmar was solely a distributor. We opened a 10,000-square-foot warehouse two blocks away from the hardware store, which we had already closed to the public. In '82, the way Wilmar worked was that I handled all the sales, marketing, and product management—so a big part of my job was knowing our products inside and out. What did I do?

I did my homework.

I truly believe knowledge is power so, like I mentioned last chapter, I became a plumbing geek. Some would say I was more like a plumbing savant, the Rain Man of plumbing! Whatever you want to call it, I was into it. There were other topics in life where I (still) couldn't tie my shoelaces, but anything in the hardware and plumbing department I would knock out of the park.

I know it doesn't sound sexy, but it served me well to know everything about the products we were selling. You could hold up a faucet stem from ten feet away, and I could tell you who made it and what year. Salespeople would walk into my office and say, "Bill, this building was built in the early 1900s. The guy gave me this as a sample. What is it?" And I'd go, "Oh, that's . . . "

I knew plumbing repair products as well as anybody else in the industry. Who cares, right? Wrong! I'll tell you, it mattered to my stakeholders, my customers, and my employees. It was proof that I wasn't some clean-desk guy who didn't get his hands dirty. My knowledge of the business proved I was invested 100 percent in my company, from top to bottom.

When my employees saw that I knew every one of our products like the back of my hand, they knew they'd better bring their A game, because I was bringing mine! I was the Chief Merchant and CEO of Wilmar/Interline Brands until the day I stepped down on Dec. 31, 2001.

This really is a great lesson for any entrepreneur who has a big product line or a complex business. Don't be a clean-desk CEO. If you're in it to win it, then prove it by doing your homework so you know your game better than anyone else.

24: I REPEAT: DO WHATEVER IT TAKES!

Okay, so we talked about adapting your business model to survive. That's huge—but there are also times in your entrepreneurial career when you want to expand your offering just to get a niche segment of clients. Why the heck would you do this? That's a trick question: most of the time, it's for the money! Other times, you might do it to corner the market on a particular service and thereby cut into the profits of your competitors.

I remember I had a few exploratory meetings with the manufacturing companies that wouldn't sell to me because Wilmar was only a distributor and wasn't marketing as a manufacturer or a repackaging company like Hancock Gross. I thought about it and determined that I wanted to be able to buy parts in bulk and package them ourselves—but that was not our business. So what did I do?

I formed a new company called Garden State Manufacturing, just so we could call these manufacturers and say we were a packaging company! Sounds like a manufacturing company to me, right? It worked. The manufacturers sold to us, and we could then buy their specialty items at the lowest possible cost.

Now, our packaging was nothing fancy, but it did the job. I had one guy that would take parts from the manufacturer, put them in a plastic bag, and seal them with a heat sealer, one at a time. Talk about manual labor, but it was effective. And when the customers got their parts, they were happy because the package was branded with the Wilmar name, our 800 number, and the item number—so reordering was easy.

This eventually led to Wilmar creating a "private label program" for many of our products, some of which became our most profitable items. I remember I created a private label faucet and showerhead line, called Wilflo faucets. (Wilflo stood for William, me, and Florence, my mom.) They didn't survive all of the acquisitions and rebrandings, but if you google "Wilflo," you'll see there are still companies who sell parts for the faucet. Another private=label creation that was a big hit for Wilmar was the BALA ceiling fan. (BALA stood for myself, Bill, and my three kids, Allison, Laura, and Adam.) They are still hot items today that can be purchased on Amazon or at retailers like Sears and WalMart.

My point with all this is, once again, I did whatever it took to get ahead. I love this motto so much, I even created gold "WIT" buttons and gave them out to employees whenever they did "Whatever It Took" to get the job done.

I wanted everyone to know I lived by these words.

I wasn't taking any shortcuts. I was building the company, even when we were small. I had a vision. Sometimes, you expand in big jumps, like adapting your business from retail to commercial—and sometimes, you do it in smaller strategic moves, like adding a packaging arm to a business. It's all about having a healthy vision and keeping your eyes on the prize.

WIT.

25: EMBRACE TECHNOLOGY AS MUCH
AS YOU CAN

Being old-school may be cool these days, but not when it comes to operating your business. You must continually embrace technology if you want your startup to soar.

Do it now. Hug your laptop, kiss your smartphone, and thank your lucky stars you're living in the 21st century. You can conquer worlds from your own home.

If you go into business and fail because you didn't invest in the best technology you could get your hands on—then I don't know what to tell you. You went into war with a water pistol, and you got soaked. Maybe next time, you will take a different approach.

If you've been cryogenically frozen for the past twenty years, let me clue you in—technology rules in today's marketplace. It doesn't matter what corner of the market you're involved in, you will have competitors who are leveraging the latest technology to take your clients.

It doesn't matter if you start a professional dog-walking service—use every technology resource you can to get those pups walked faster, better, and more efficiently. I may not be Bill Gates, Elon Musk, or Mark Zuckerberg, but trust me on this one!

I speak from experience. I absolutely love technology, always have. I wanted to automate and computerize before personal computers even existed. I was doing things in the '80s that companies are doing today. Remember, I wanted to be a one-stop-shop, so at every stage of my career, I've used the latest technology to connect with customers, improve our operations, tailor our touchpoints, and provide better customer service. I did it with Wilmar back in the day, and I'm doing it with LendingOne now.

I remember the first time Wilmar went digital—we bought a mainframe! It was 1984. We had two branches and were doing $2.7 million in sales. So I stepped up and dropped $50,000 on a mainframe computer called a Digital Equipment PDP-11/23 Plus. It was cutting-edge technology and only had 500K of storage capacity. I remember, because a year later we upgraded to a mainframe with one gig.

I know, even the worst smartphone on earth has one gig,

right? But a gigabyte was a big deal back in 1985.

Jump ahead to 1992: the Internet was still incubating. We were still living in the Dark Ages—customers either had to call or fax in their orders. But I knew there was a better way. I remember envisioning our customers being able to go on a computer in their office and put their own orders into our system.

I looked around and found a good deal on a Wyse WY50 terminal, so I bought ten for some of my customers. Then I stopped by their offices and installed them for free. They weren't even our ten biggest clients; they were just ones that I knew had dial-up modems and would bring us more business if they could place orders this way.

I told them, "This is going to save you time, so I'm going to put this terminal in your office that connects to our main computer." And they loved it. You better believe those ten customers became "super sticky." And they were even more loyal and prolific after I empowered them with new technology.

Looking back, those first ten computer terminals were the beginning of super-differentiating ourselves from our competitors. No other businesses I knew of were giving their customers terminals. Nobody. Zero. Zilch. It was just another huge step in improving our customer service.

MY DAD REJECTED TECHNOLOGY

Of course, not everyone in our company embraced technology the way I did. Boy, did my dad fight me every step of the way! His stance on technology was the beginning of the end for Dad's career, because he pushed back so hard that we both realized he would never change, and the times were starting to pass him by.

I love him, but looking back, his technophobia was fairly comical. He was adamant about not wanting to deal with a computer. He wouldn't even turn one on!

I'd say, "Dad, we have fifty of these widgets in stock."

He'd say, "Well, I'm going to go back and count them."

I'd tell him that we had inventory software for that and he would say, "I don't believe what the computer says."

I remember when I installed a perpetual inventory system.

I'd say, "Dad, look, the computer's telling us to buy a hundred faucets."

He'd say, "That's not the way you do it. You have the vendor come in, and they walk around the warehouse and look in the bin and they tell you what you need. That's the way it works."

I'd say, "Dad, that's nuts when you can do it on the computer!"

He'd go, "Computer schmooter."

This is what I had to live with! And it drove me crazy because I was a tech geek. I couldn't get enough of technology. As soon as something new came out, I wanted it.

I remember having to fight him on everything. I'd say we needed a Telex machine after we started importing from Taiwan, and he would complain.

I'd say, "Dad, we need to get an 800 number."

He'd say, "Tell the customers to call collect."

I remember saying, "Dad, we need to buy a fax machine."

He'd say, "They're six thousand dollars!" That one was a battle for months.

Sometimes, I'd catch Dad on a good day. I remember in 1984 when Apple had just released the first Macintosh that had this new software called Adobe PageMaker. I said, "Dad, I can't cut and paste text anymore; I want to buy one of these Macs."

Amazingly, he said, "Okay, let's go."

I had caught him in a good mood! So we both walked into Jonathan's Computer Store and put down ten thousand bucks.

That's what a Mac cost back then.

I eventually won the tech war with good old Dad. I know he would never admit it, even today, but investing in technology was one of the smartest moves we ever made. It raised the performance of every ship in our fleet—and was absolutely the right thing to do for our business. It certainly is for yours.

I guarantee it.

26: FIGHT FOR YOUR RIGHT TO GROW

Running your own business can be a real thrill ride—but it can also be a battle and sometimes a flat-out war. Some of your trusted lieutenants may run for cover when artillery fire starts whizzing by your head. But if you're a leader who has a great strategy and an awesome weapon and has managed to "keep your powder dry," don't tuck tail and run just because your business partners don't have the courage and vision you have.

Keep charging.

I'm speaking from experience. I had to fight my business partner (Dad) for everything I wanted to do on the growth front. Once we got to a certain level, Dad was the tortoise, and I was the hare; he wanted to stay put while I kept charging ahead like General MacArthur taking hill after hill.

Dad would tell me I was crazy so many times, I started to tune him out. I didn't let his fear of losing it all quash my dreams. Once we got rolling, I knew we had something great going, so I never questioned myself; I'd just smile and say, "Dad, I love you—but we're doing it my way."

I fought for what I believed in, and I was right.

If you have that same gut instinct, don't be afraid to keep pushing your business into the future. There will always be naysayers who are going to tell you, "It can't be done." Sometimes the people holding the "caution flag" are your friends, business partners, or mentors—and sometimes, they're right. So be smart, and do your homework. Bravery can get you killed if you don't know what you're doing.

But also keep in mind that anything worth doing in life—starting your own business, getting married, having kids, or buying a house—has some kind of risk attached to it. Anything you try could crash and burn, but that doesn't mean you should play defense your whole life—how boring would that be?

DARING TO CAST A WIDER NET

By 1984, I was playing offense. I was feeling it. I was knocking down shots like Dr. J! Wilmar was starting to get really well-known in the Delaware Valley. By now, all our customers were the maintenance departments of apartment buildings—many of which were owned and operated by management companies that had multiple properties all over the East Coast.

So one day, I befriended this guy who was doing large

apartment complex renovations, not far from us. We got to talking, and he said, "You know, Bill, we're doing the same kind of renovations in Columbia, Maryland. If you guys open up a warehouse there, we'll buy your stuff there, too."

That got me to thinking—why not cast a wider net? Maryland seemed like a great opportunity, right? We'd have instant business there, so why not?

I went to Dad and pitched him my idea.

He said, "No way, no."

I couldn't believe it. No matter how much I tried to explain it to him, he just didn't grasp my grand vision. We were at loggerheads. Here we were, doing $2.7 million in annual sales. Dad and I were only paying ourselves salaries of $40,000 a year, and he didn't want to rock the boat? I said, "C'mon, Dad, we haven't reached our ceiling—we can do better than this."

Dad said, "Billy, you've lost your mind."

As you might guess, I didn't listen. I went rogue. I didn't let the possibility of failure scare me into stasis.

I was on a mission.

I drove down to Columbia and found a real estate agent, and just like that, I opened up a 5,000-square-foot warehouse on my own. Dad was against it, but I believed in myself. Boy, was it hard opening up that branch. The first year, we lost money. You should've heard Dad howl, "Billy, you screwed up!" But I said, "Just give it time." So I kept working at it, and guess what?

A year and a half later, that one branch became wildly profitable. Ten years later, that one branch was bringing in $25 million a year in revenue! And Columbia, Maryland is still one of Wilmar/Interline's biggest regions to this day.

So I knocked down another clutch fourth-quarter shot for the home team. Think I got a high five from Dad when I came back to the huddle? If you said "yes," you haven't been reading! I love my dad, but he really is a tough guy. He's not a Gemini, but he should be! He could be the sweetest, nicest guy in the world and then a second later be as tough as nails.

I remember I used to play basketball on Saturdays as a kid in a township league. Dad rarely came to my games, but one of the few times he did, I scored nineteen points.

Want to know what he said to me after the game?

"You played terrible defense."

I never figured him out. He's an enigma wrapped inside a puzzle. I don't think Dad intentionally did anything to hurt us; he just didn't know how to treat kids. He simply wasn't wired that way. Nothing was ever good enough, but that motivated me. Maybe that was why he always pushed back on my aspirations, to motivate me—if so, it sure as hell worked!

27: BE PERSISTENT AND CONSISTENT

Dad never said, "Great job, Billy." He was from the old school where the only compliments "real men" ever gave were at people's funerals! Here's my favorite Dad story that really exemplifies the way he motivated me. It also ties into a lesson I taught myself.

Back in the early days, there were these two apartment complexes in Marlton, pretty close to each other, the Alison Apartments and Hunter's Run. And for one reason or another, I was never able to get their business. It drove me nuts because they were in my hometown, but I never gave up.

Every two weeks, I'd stop in to see the managers of the apartments. I remember the manager of the Alison Apartments was named Marian. She kept telling me the same thing: they only bought from Pier Angeli.

Pier Angeli, Pier Angeli—I heard that name in my sleep!

This went on for years. But I'm no quitter, and you can't be either, if you're serious about business or life. You have to be dogged in your pursuit of your goals when it comes to anything you want. You can't be lazy and expect to get ahead.

Drill it into your head: be persistent and consistent.

I kept at it. Then one day, I paid Marian a visit, and as luck would have it, Pier Angeli had just screwed up one of her orders. She said, "Bill, come into my office," and she gave me my first order. Awesome, right?

I called Dad to tell him the news from a 7-Eleven pay phone, and you know what he said?

"Did you get Hunter's Run yet?"

That's a perfect example of Dad.

DAD HANDED ME A BRICK, AND
I BUILT A HOUSE

I can't make it sound like Dad didn't teach me anything, because you've got to understand that when I started out, I knew nothing. I like to say my dad handed me a brick, and I built a house. Dad taught me the ropes; he shared his connections in the business with me and taught me, "It's not what you know. It's who you know," which is so true.

I remember there was this guy that worked for a property management company who used to walk into the hardware store and say, "I'd like to buy more from you, but until you're an approved vendor, I can't."

"How do I become an approved vendor?" I asked.

The guy said I had to go see Sid Cohen. So I called Sid Cohen, who was kind of a gruff guy, and I asked him how I could become an approved vendor.

And he said, "Come to my office, and we'll talk about it."

So I told Dad, "I have an appointment with Sid Cohen. I don't know what to say." Dad taught me a great lesson about sales that day.

He said, "When you go into his office, don't talk about business right away. Try to get friendly with him first."

Sounded like pretty good advice—so I took it.

I walked into Sid Cohen's office, and I was nervous as hell. I wasn't more than eighteen. I sat down in the chair across from his desk and saw pictures of his kid holding a baseball bat.

So I said, "Oh, is that your son?"

"Yeah, that's my son," Sid said.

"He plays baseball?"

Sid and I started talking about baseball. The guy happened to be a former New Yorker, so I asked him, "Mets or Yankees?"

And he said, "Mets."

I said, "I'm a Mets fan, too; I was born in Brooklyn. My parents moved here when I was four, but I'm still a Mets fan," and we just started a dialogue about baseball.

The rest was history. I made a personal connection with the guy. From that moment on, it felt like we were two friendly guys talking instead of two strangers with nothing in common.

The next thing you know, I became an approved vendor, thanks to Sid. That's a scene right out of *How to Win Friends and Influence People*, right? One of the best books ever. And Dad taught me that lesson when I was eighteen.

All these years later, I want to give my dad a pat on the back for all the things he did to help me—even though he probably wouldn't do the same for me if his life depended on it.

BUYING THE REST OF THE BUSINESS

Fast-forward to 1986: Dad semiretired and bought a condo in Florida. He started flying south for the winter with Mom two years later. I'd send them monthly financials, but I was running the business and doing all the work.

We were rolling without him. By 1988, we were generating $10 million in sales. I began hiring other salespeople (mostly my friends) in 1982, but now we had forty employees and a third branch in Houston, Texas.

I wasn't content.

My new obsession became getting national accounts. I had a knack for making friends and showing clients why it was better for them to buy from us in a one-stop shop scenario. I'd give them our value proposition: I'd say we sold everything, had great prices, delivered next day, and gave them one invoice. And of course, our secret sauce was our great customer service.

One day, I looked around at what I created and said, "Man, now we're real!"

So I said to my parents, "Here's the deal. Since you guys are basically retired and I'm the rainmaker on every side of the business, I want you to gift me enough stock so I'm a 51 percent owner of the company." So they did.

Then in 1990, I told them I wanted to buy the rest of the business. "Where are you going to get the money?" Dad asked. I didn't know. I was only paying myself $120,000 a year. I had bought a nice house; I had a wife, two kids. I thought I was rich, but I didn't have any money in the bank.

I'd put it all back into the business.

28: MAKE YOUR BUSINESS A PIGGY BANK, NOT A CASH COW

I was in this liquidity dilemma—but looking back, I feel my rationale was sound. I still believe to this day that, when you are starting your own company—it doesn't matter how profitable you are out of the gate—you should keep putting what you earn back into growing your business. You're going to get paid eventually if you keep grinding, but don't loot the treasury and start living like a king before the paint's dry on your kingdom.

Except for our relatively modest salaries, Dad and I never took any money out of Wilmar; that's one of the things that differentiated us from a lot of our competitors that I eventually acquired.

Think about it: if you are truly in it to win it, you have to put your money where your bread is buttered, and that's back into your business. So many entrepreneurs don't get this.

Almost every business I acquired was way smaller than us, but the funny thing was, their CEOs were paying themselves these huge salaries. In 1997, after we'd gone public, I was interested in buying this company based in Detroit that had $25 million in sales. The two owners were paying themselves annual salaries of $600,000 each.

And they couldn't understand why they weren't able to grow their company! Duh. When I was a $25 million company, I paid myself $150,000. Do the math. They were paying 5 percent of their annual sales to themselves (2.5 percent each)! When I bought their company, they wanted to come work for me—but it didn't work out.

Want to know why? I wouldn't pay them enough.

I had been putting money back into our business for the past thirteen years. I didn't have the cash to buy Dad out, so I said to him, "Just tell me how much you want, and I'll figure it out."

Dad said, "I want two million bucks for the other half of the business."

I said, "Okay. I'll find a way to get the money."

It took three years to close that deal!

But by 1993, I was able to get it inked. I gave my parents a couple of million dollars to get the transfer of ownership. And there I was—with complete ownership of a $35 million company that I started from a pile of unwanted parts at a flea market. We were making $3.5 million in profits, and I was still only taking a $150,000 salary.

I call it bootstrapping a startup.

Those early years were a wild roller-coaster ride. I fought, I scrapped, I took enemy fire, and kept taking hill after hill. I picked up customers and vendors, and built a team of employees one by one through persistency, relationships, and pounding the pavement.

By 1993, we finally had a corporate home I was really proud of. I bought Wilmar's first official corporate headquarters in Moorestown, New Jersey.

What a journey it had taken to get this far. Our new home was a 13,000-square-foot office building in a beautiful office park in a very nice area. Now we had a large conference room, columns in the lobby, and a skylight in the main foyer. It was a big step up from our old digs and sure beat sleeping in the backseat of my dad's car in a flea market's parking lot!

We now had six branches all over the country: New Jersey, Maryland, Texas, Indiana, California, and Georgia.

Wilmar had arrived.

29: THINK BIG, ACT BIG, AND YOU WILL BE BIG

How did I go from a kid with a startup to a CEO in fifteen years? I think it had something to do with this lesson, what I call the "brainy cousin" of lesson #5: "Look successful, act successful, and you'll be successful." But this lesson takes it to the next level.

Anyone can look the part, but that's only half the battle. Now you have to think and act the part, and I'm not just talking about believing in yourself. I'm talking about conceptualizing your dream in real, actionable terms and then making it happen.

You want to be big, okay—how are you going to get there? You have to construct the bridge to greatness in your mind before you can do anything. See what I mean? I not only looked the part and believed in myself, but I also thought bigger than I really was my entire life.

Here's a good example. Remember the plumbing supply company Pier Angeli? I was a nothing little guy when I first picked up their catalogue, right? I remember thinking, "Man, they're doing what I want to do." So I set my sights on them. I thought big. I remember telling Dad back at the hardware store, "I want to be like Pier Angeli one day." Boy, would he laugh. Dad would say, "You're not a pimple on their ass, kid. Stop dreaming." It almost made me cry to hear him say that—so you can imagine I was motivated as hell to prove him wrong one day.

ANOTHER DREAM COMES TRUE

Fast-forward to 1997, and guess what? I bought Pier Angeli. By then, we had cut into so much of their customer base, Pier Angeli had shrunk from an $18 million company in its heyday to a $4 million company. It felt great; I was really excited about the deal.

I drove over to tell Dad the news. When you buy a company, your investment banker gives you a Lucite standing plaque to commemorate the deal.

I walked in the door and dropped the Pier Angeli plaque on his lap.

Dad said, "What's this?"

"That's the pimple on my ass, Dad."

KEY TAKEAWAYS

- Always keep your eyes on the prize.
- Keep putting money in your business—it's crucial to continued growth.
- Think big, act big, but never forget your roots.
- Never settle—keep setting new goals as you reach old ones.
- Create a niche for your business, and don't try to be the low-cost king; it doesn't pay off.

- Keep adapting and reinvesting in your business.
- Embrace technology—it's the way of the future, and understanding how it works will help your business succeed.

CHAPTER 5

IT'S ALL ABOUT THE CUSTOMER

*There is only one boss, the customer, and he can fire
everybody from the chairman on down by simply
bringing his business somewhere else.*

—Sam Walton, founder, Walmart and Sam's Club

I REALLY ENJOY dealing with customers. Simply put, I love them, and for good reason. In the business world, they are our everything. How you treat them is so vital to your future success, I'm dedicating an entire chapter to them. They are that important.

The customers are our unsung heroes; they are the ones who stoke our creative embers and fuel our financial fire. If you don't have your eye on the client experience every minute of every day, you're completely missing the point of why you are in business. Without them in your corner, any venture you start may as well be a very expensive vanity project, because you're only doing it for yourself.

Have you ever heard the phrase "be the ball" in sports? If you want to knock down shots in the customer service arena, you have to "be the client."

In one word, you should treat them like *family*.

30: CREATE AN ARMY OF RAVING FANS

If you want to be a huge hit out of the gate, you need to work on creating an army of raving fans. I'm not saying start a cult-like following—but try to start a cult-like following!

This is not an original Coach Green adage; it was coined by a guy named Ken Blanchard, who wrote a great book, *Raving Fans: A Revolutionary Approach to Customer Service*. When I read this book, I realized that is how I had already been treating my customers, so I officially instilled his motto into the culture of all my businesses from there on out.

No matter how big or how small you are, all the best companies do it.

Look at a company like Apple. Once people buy their first Mac or iPhone, they're hooked, right? You rarely see people go back to PCs even though Macs have their flaws. Why?

Because Apples aren't just products to their customers—they are a lifestyle choice. Even now, after the golden Jobs era has passed, their customers still love them in an almost irrational way. They don't just want them; they think they need them.

That's the kind of fervent loyalty you want to inspire in your customers. Make them so crazy for you that they can't live without you.

31: LEARN YOUR CLIENTS' WANTS AND NEEDS

How do you create raving fans of your work? You can start by giving them a lot of tender loving care. When I say "Treat your clients like family," I don't mean treat them like a second cousin who you never see. Treat them like your spouse. I'm also not saying let them move into your house or sleep in your bed, but you have to yearn to get into their heads like they were someone you really care about understanding.

You don't make assumptions about what your spouse wants to do on his or her birthday. You care enough to spend time picking out the perfect gift (or thing to do) to show them that you love them, right? You better have that same sense of urgency when it comes to understanding your customers, or you're not going to please anyone—including yourself.

If you are just starting out, spend some time and resources understanding your customers before you launch your business. You can start by asking yourself questions like these:

1. Who are my clients?
2. Why would they buy from me instead of someone else?
3. How are their needs going to evolve?
4. How can I stay on their permanent wish list?
5. If I were a customer, what would perfection look like to me?

Just like dealing with your spouse, never assume you know the answer to anything! Gather evidence that proves it. I'm not talking about sending out a few customer surveys or focus-testing your new product on a small group of customers. I'm talking about collecting a large sample size of unbiased, quantifiable data.

One snapshot isn't going to do it. Why? The modern customer is always evolving, especially now with technology being such a huge part of our lives. Nothing remains static anymore, so your value proposition and customer experience have to evolve, or you're going to end up like Blockbuster Video before you know what Netflix truck hit you.

32: IF YOU'RE TALKING, YOU'RE NOT LISTENING

It may sound like a cliché, but keep your finger on the pulse of your industry. If you don't feel you're savvy enough to do it, find someone to be your barometer. But no matter what, you can't delegate the client experience entirely.

To be a successful entrepreneur, you have to have an emotional connection to your clients. It can't all be based on cold impersonal transactions—there has to be some kind of bond at the center of it all. To foster this bond, you have to get out there and meet them yourself. Don't let your ego stand in the way of doing your job. Get out of your ivory tower, and hit the streets, pound the pavement, and slap some hands!

Talk to your customers like they are your friends.

Don't talk at them—have a real conversation with them. Look them in the eye, and listen to what they have to say. Prick up your ears. It's amazing what you can find out when you aren't just waiting for your chance to talk.

It's crazy, but so many CEOs have these huge egos and think they know more than they do. Hey, there's nothing wrong with having confidence, but overconfidence can get in the way of hearing honest feedback. If I'm describing you or maybe one of your business partners, let me tell you—so much of success is based on timing and luck.

So deflate those big heads, and stay humble. You are always at the service of your clients, no matter how big you get. Don't just take it from me. Look at guys like Bill Gates, Sam Walton, or Charles Schwab—they're billionaires who never got too big to attribute all their success to the people who deserve it.

The Greeks call having a big ego "hubris," and from the beginning of time to now, it's always been a problem for the successful. It not only clouds your judgment—it can taint any customer data you try to collect. How?

I've seen a lot of CEOs doing "client outreach" who end up talking to customers like they're politicians on the campaign trail. These guys love hearing the sound of their own voice, so the conversations are one-sided. Whenever they hear a keyword come out of a customer's mouth, the CEO pivots into a talking point. So what are they learning here? Nothing new. Don't you see? It's like cooking the books on customer feedback. These guys never learn anything other than stuff that validates what they think they already know.

When doing customer outreach, leave your ego at the door, and get real so your customers can get real with you. That way you can collect some real, raw, and useful information that isn't skewed to any preconceived assumption.

33: GOOD CUSTOMERS COMPLAIN, BAD CUSTOMERS GO AWAY

Some CEOs with fragile egos may tighten up when they run into a customer who is passionately unhappy, but those customers are gold. They're gifts! Pay attention to passion, even if their passion is anger. Take it as a compliment; it means they care enough about your product that it angers them not to have it.

I've heard from a lot of business owners who say to me, "Why aren't we getting more business? The customers aren't calling."

I'll ask, "Do you know why?"

And they have no idea. I'm thinking, *Maybe it's your service!*

Of course, I never tell them that. I just say, "You know, just because your customers aren't telling you that you're giving them bad service doesn't mean you're not giving them bad service."

The good ones complain; the bad ones just go away.

Let me illustrate: if you have a bad meal at a lousy restaurant, do you tell the owner about it? No, you just go away. Now, let's say you go to your favorite restaurant and have a bad experience. You're shocked, right? You're hurt. You can't believe it. You're probably going to say something, because you love that restaurant so much. You want them to fix it so you can keep coming back and enjoying the food.

I know this from personal experience. I've invested in five restaurants throughout my career. My first was in Marlton. The food was amazing, but it was plagued with bad customer service. I remember every time a friend would tell me about a bad experience, I'd ask my operating partner about it, and boy, would I hear excuses. "Oh, they came late," or "They took too long to order and made so many changes."

It would drive me nuts. I'd say, "Stop blaming the customer!"

Well, guess what? That restaurant went out of business.

I believe so much in the power of "the customer is always right" mindset that I've ingrained it deep into the culture of every one of my businesses, and it's worked. Even to this day, if I hear about an unhappy customer, I see to it that his or her problem is fixed—then, boom! Suddenly, that raving mad customer is back to being a raving fan of our work.

34: FIX MISTAKES FAST

That wasn't the last time I worked with people who tried to blame the customer. Repeat after me: it's never their fault. When trouble hits, don't be defensive about it. Don't run around trying to assign blame. Just fall on your sword and do whatever it takes to fix it fast.

This should be obvious, but in this PC era when no one wants to call anybody out because they're afraid of hurting someone's feelings, accountability can be passed around like a hot potato until no one remembers who dropped the ball in the first place.

I don't count the screw-ups as much as I keep tabs on how quickly problems are resolved. I always tell my people, "We're all human, and we're going to make mistakes. But the customer is going to remember how fast you fix the problem more than they're going to remember the mistake itself."

So if you screw up a customer order and they complain— then two hours later, the rest of their order shows up on their doorstep—guess what? Odds are good they will forget they were raving mad and only remember they are raving fans again.

35: BE CREATIVE,
BE AN UNDERCOVER BOSS

This stuff isn't something I made up. I spent years of my life researching how customers think. This project has been a lifelong passion that I'm continuing with my new business, LendingOne, which I started after spending time as a real estate investor.

I was looking for financing for these properties I owned, and I noticed how lousy the customer service was by the companies providing the loans to investors like myself. It was so terrible that I thought, *I can do better than this,* so that's exactly what I'm doing with LendingOne.

You really have to find a way to put yourself in your customer's shoes, even when it's not something you would do in your everyday life.

Back when I was running Wilmar and our day-to-day clients were property owners and the maintenance managers who worked for them, I wanted to see what their lives were like. For two weeks, I took a night job working in a high-rise apartment building that one of my customers owned. After my day job as CEO of Wilmar was through, I became a different kind of undercover boss, except I wasn't infiltrating my own company; I was inhabiting the world of our customers.

It was quite a revelation.

I'd get the work order, go down to the shop, and look for the parts. Then I'd knock on a tenant's door and say, "Hi, I'm Bill from maintenance." I was even dressed like a maintenance man.

Ironically, even though I was a plumbing savant, I'm not a great "fixit" guy, so I will admit I was never 100 percent successful, but I was able to make simple faucet repairs, fix a few leaky toilets, and change a few lightbulbs.

It was a great experience, because it helped me understand what the maintenance man had to go through. New things were always coming up that I would never have known about if I hadn't experienced them.

For example, I learned maintenance men could fix anything but weren't very good at controlling their inventory. I noticed they'd run out of stuff, so I went out of my way to make their lives easier and help them get organized. Remember, these people typically had small shops; using expensive technology to track inventory would have been impractical. So we provided a service where our field sales reps would help maintenance men organize their storage shops and create order points, so when their inventory of a specific item got down to a certain point, it reminded them to order more.

The big lesson here is to find creative ways to put yourself in your customer's shoes; it can really help the evolution of your value proposition.

36: UNDERPROMISE, OVERDELIVER

I don't want to speak out of school, because I love entrepreneurs, but I've noticed a lot of us can be real pains! Call us type-A, go-getting perfectionists, but a lot of us have a very specific vision for how things should be done. You see it all the time; it's why some of us have the DNA to do what we do in the first place.

You may demand perfection from yourself, your partners, and your employees—but you can't let that carry over to how you talk to your customers. Don't promise perfection to them. Just don't. I know in this modern age, ideally, everything should be perfect all the time, right? We live in the age of airbrushed and Photoshopped celebrities—but that's not reality. That's TV and the movies. Nobody's doing things perfectly all the time. It's never happened in the history of business; it's never happened in the history of anything!

You can aspire to be infallible, but it's going to cost you. And before you start making promises you can't keep, you should ask yourself, "Is it worth it?" You can pay out the wazoo to be really close to perfect, but even then, you can't eliminate all bugs from your operation. You just can't.

Because I'm a guy who's always striving to deliver the perfect customer service experience, it should come as no surprise that I thought about this a lot when I was running Wilmar. We were moving a huge volume of merchandise, and we strived for 97 percent fill rates. I did my homework and determined that, sure, we could have targeted a 99 percent fill rate—but do you know what the cost of those extra two percentage points would have been in inventory dollars?

It would have been mind-boggling. Not to mention impractical, when you have fifteen thousand items and have to manage your balance sheet.

If you're operating in a high-volume business, you have to determine a perfection ratio that works best for you. The smart thing to do is to make reasonable promises to your customers and then overdeliver on your promise. There is something about human nature that loves the pleasant surprise. When you do it even better than what they expected, they love you for it.

And as I said earlier, loyal customers will forgive a mistake if you fix it fast!

37: BE MULTILOCAL: THINK NATIONALLY, ACT LOCALLY

You've heard of the Greenpeace slogan, "Think globally, act locally," right? Same thing goes for the world of business. Once

Wilmar became a national company with multiple locations coast to coast, we realized very quickly that we needed to think nationally and act locally.

From all my client research, I noticed virtually every client and vendor I got to know said they would prefer to do business with someone local. No one wants to deal with a faceless national company; they want to deal with a familiar friend. They just do. They trust a local face and especially trust a local voice.

After we found this out, we tailored all our touchpoints to our customers' individual preference. If a person liked to do business on the phone, we called him or her. If they liked in-person meetings, we'd have one of our field sales reps visit them.

We even developed specialty brands dedicated to a specific customer's buying patterns. For example, I noticed we had a lot of customers who needed minimal help purchasing, so we created Supply Depot, just for them. Supply Depot was all mail order and offered the lowest possible prices. We later integrated Supply Depot into a company we acquired, Maintenance USA.

How were we able to offer such low prices? Do the math. We didn't have to employ any field reps!

38: TAILOR YOUR EXPERIENCE TO THE CUSTOMER

This is a hugely important lesson in today's market. You can't make customers adjust to you anymore; those days are over. You have to tailor your experience to them, and make them feel like part of your family.

I remember that once we had our Houston branch up and running, we noticed Texans didn't like talking to our New Jersey-based customer service representatives. Want to know why? Because they thought we were a bunch of carpetbagging Yankees! Some traditions die hard.

Texans, by and large, wanted to hear a Southern voice when they called us. Being fanatical about customer service, I decided to create regional customer service centers all over the country. This is done all over the place today, but we were way ahead of the curve back in the '90s. None of our competitors was doing it like we were.

I even invested a million dollars in a phone system that would funnel calls to the appropriate region—so when somebody called from a specific area code, it went to their regional office. In Houston, we hired locals to answer the phones so their background and accents were familiar to our Texas clients.

Of course, certain aspects like accounting and collections had to stay centralized, but we kept a local touchpoint for those parts of the business as well. If customers called from the Houston area and needed to talk to somebody in accounting, they would first speak to a representative in our Houston regional call center.

Our reps would say, "Hold on; I'm going to transfer you to Mary in accounting." Mary would be in New Jersey. But because our customers' first impression felt local, their guard went down, and they didn't know or care that they were talking to a Yankee on the East Coast.

I know what you might be saying: "You really spent a million dollars on a phone system?" No, I spent a million dollars on customer service!

Remember, this was before VoIP (Voice over Internet Protocol) was even invented. Back then, you had to invest in a phone system if you were a national company that wanted to seamlessly connect with clients across the country.

This seamless connectivity also allowed me to hire the best people.

Here's a good example. I had this great product support guy who was living in Detroit. But he didn't want to move to our headquarters in New Jersey, so instead of losing him to one of our competitors, I said, "You know what? Stay put in Detroit, and we'll just funnel customers your way through our phone system."

The whole thing was seamless for the customer, and it worked great. That's one investment that really stood up over time.

DATABASE MANAGEMENT FOR BETTER CUSTOMER SERVICE

That wasn't all we did to make our customers feel like they were talking to family. When a customer who was in our system called in to our regional customer service centers, our database automatically pulled up the customer's account history before one of our representatives even answered the phone.

Our system not only gave our reps the customer's entire purchasing history, at the end of the call, it also prompted them to say things like, "Hey, Joe, I see you bought twenty showerheads last month; are you running low?" Or "I see you bought three cases of lightbulbs. If you've run out, they're on special this month."

We weren't trying to item-upsell and get them to buy a more expensive product. We also weren't trying to order-upsell and get customers to buy larger quantities of stuff. What we did was suggestive sales based on past purchases.

A lot of times, just mentioning their past purchasing history would prompt responses like "Oh yeah, I do need more of those. Thanks for reminding me!" That was all database management. Being able to pull data up in real time just as the phone rang was pretty big.

I have no idea what type of business you are in. It doesn't matter. This is a universal lesson I'm teaching you here: to endear yourself to your customers, customize all your touchpoints so they feel like they are talking to family.

It's a winning formula: yesterday, today, and tomorrow.

39: MAKE YOUR TRANSACTION MODEL EASIER THAN YOUR COMPETITION'S

Our customer-centric mindset also influenced how we created the Wilmar catalogues. Every year, they got bigger and better. At one point, after we had installed our database, we knew exactly what each customer had bought from us (it was all in our system), so I thought, since maintenance men aren't great at inventory control, why don't we make their job easier by creating specialized catalogues—and literally give them their own buying list?

Just like that, we started offering customers two catalogues. Everybody got the master catalogue, and if you wanted one, you also got your own specific buying list catalogue. We also backed that with the Wilmar website, where you could go to your buying history and do a quick order.

I'm also doing the same thing with the LendingOne website. Borrowers can see everything related to their loans online, while our loan officers can manage the borrowers' online experience and provide advice along the way.

My goal with all this customization is to let my customers know "Your wish is our command." That became one of Wilmar's marketing slogans, but it was all about making the customer's life easier.

Repeat after me: "Do Whatever It Takes." What is that Mark Cuban quote? "Make your product easier to buy than your competition's, or you will find your customers buying from them, not you." It's so true, now more than ever.

If you aren't doing everything you possibly can to bend over backwards to make your clients' life easier in this age of one-stop shopping, then get ready to become a museum piece!

PEOPLE LOVE SAME-DAY SERVICE

Back at Wilmar, we had this local competitor in Texas that started offering same-day delivery. I noticed after a while we were starting to lose business to them because we weren't offering the same thing. I thought about it and said, "Okay, let's offer same-day delivery too."

Pretty bold move, right? Some of my team thought I'd lost my mind.

Then I doubled down and said, "You know what? Let's start doing it everywhere, not just Texas." So we started offering it in all our other regions. Man, our national competitors were going crazy scrambling to keep up!

You want to know a little secret? The offer worked like gangbusters, but the crazy thing was, nobody was taking advantage of it. The customers just wanted the peace of mind of knowing that, if they needed it, they could get it the same day.

Just giving them the option kept them loyal and threw a monkey wrench into our competitors' operations. It was also a little bit of psychological warfare—you have to get into competitors' heads!

It was also one of the best marketing tools we ever pulled off.

If I had bitten off more than I could chew and hadn't organized it right, it could have cost us a fortune. But I did my homework. I understood most maintenance men aren't going to call in before 10 a.m. with a rush order—they were just getting their head turned by a competitor who offered it. So I went all in.

If you do your homework and decide a bold move would drive your competition crazy, you'll get major efficiencies by showing your customers that you'll do whatever it takes to give them peace of mind. And when you can make a bold move that pleases your customer and screws with the heads of your competition?

That's killing two birds with one stone.

40: SURVIVAL OF THE FITTEST: ADAPT TO ADVANCE

Speaking of psychological warfare, business can get bloody. Guts can fly everywhere: it's the law of the jungle. You have to accept that fact before jumping into the line of fire. It doesn't matter what kind of demeanor you have in real life. In the world of business, you must have the heart for the fight.

You can't get squeamish when it's go time. Just look at me. If you met me at a dinner party, you'd probably say, "Bill is a nice guy," but when it comes to business, I've got my game face on at all times.

You have to be merciless to win in this dog-eat-dog world. That's why they call it survival of the fittest. This means if your competition falls down and screws up, you've got to step on their necks. If you let them live to fight another day, boy, can it come back and haunt you. Don't let an opportunity to kill off a competitor pass you by.

When I was at Wilmar, whenever we heard a competitor lost a sales rep in a specific region, I'd go for the jugular—we'd do a team sales blitz. I'd ask every sales rep I had in that region to make a call to every potential customer as quickly as possible; I'd even fly reps in to back them up.

Heartless? Ruthless? Yes and yes. Step on their necks. Take their customers.

Don't be naïve; every single one of your competitors would step on yours in a heartbeat. If you're feeling queasy about it, take some Kaopectate.

This is the big stage; don't get stage fright now. That's why they call it show business, not show friendship.

I'LL SAY IT AGAIN: KEEP ADAPTING

You can't stay still on customer service. You have to keep adapting your business model again and again to sustain it. You have to be on a mission to please, at all times. Never slow down!

It's so tough to maintain success just as a low-cost provider, but if you can whip up some of that secret sauce and create a business that offers fair prices and outstanding customer service? It's always going to be a winner.

Remember, "Get 'em on price; keep 'em on service."

But having a bunch of great customer service programs is only one part of the equation. You have to make your people believe it. It can't just be window dressing.

Every employee you hire must buy into it, and "drink the Kool-Aid"—and they can only do that if they follow the example from the top. This is exactly what I've done with every single business I've been involved with, and that's sure as heck what I'm doing with LendingOne.

Think about it: LendingOne is a fintech company, so who do you think our competitors are? They are companies whose CEOs are typically coders and tech guys! These guys don't have a lot of experience creating a customer-first culture. The concept is so foreign to them. They are hiring people to be their customer-service experience chiefs instead of pushing that culture down from the top, which is what I'm doing.

When it comes down to us versus them, who would you bet on to provide the best customer experience?

I know who I'm putting my money on.

KEY TAKEAWAYS

- Build a dedicated fan base, and you'll have customers for life.
- Find out what your clients need, and give it to them by listening to them.
- Good customers complain—turn them into raving fans.
- Build a culture around great customer service.
- Fix problems fast, and investigate your company by putting yourself in your clients' shoes.
- You may aspire to perfection, but it isn't reasonable. Instead, underpromise and overdeliver.
- Listen, don't talk. If you're talking, you're not learning how to make your company better.

CHAPTER 6

BUILDING A CHAMPIONSHIP TEAM

Customer service is not a department. It's everyone's job.

—Ken Blanchard, author and management expert

AT THIS POINT, it's fair to say you've got a decent idea of how to build a company that fills a niche in the marketplace, how to attract customers and keep them, and how to maintain the right attitude throughout the process. If you've done all those things, you're on the right track to building a successful business with longevity.

But there's the question of who to have on your team. Building the right team is critical to future success. You may have a wonderful product and excel at delivering client needs, but you're sunk if your team doesn't have the same enthusiasm, drive, or values that you have. In this chapter, I'll explain why it's important to have a winning team on your side, and how to build a great group of employees who are just as dedicated to your business as you are.

41: SURROUND YOURSELF WITH WINNERS

If you ever have an opportunity to spend some time with a really successful entrepreneur or CEO, pay close attention. I did.

When I was starting out, I'd pick their brains and take notes.

One thing I learned after meeting a lot of them is that the most successful ones are passionate about their business and can do it all extremely well. These CEOs are the total package: all-around players who can shoot, rebound, play defense, and handle the ball. That's what makes them hall-of-famers.

I've also met quite a few entrepreneurs and CEOs who got fired or ran their company into the ground. What do the "less successful ones" have in common? I think a lot of them share a fatal flaw that no one tells them about. Why? Because they surround themselves with yes-men and women who won't give it to them straight.

Guess what? That's their fatal flaw.

A lot of these "less successful" top dogs have this destructive tendency not to hire anybody smarter than them. I don't get it. Maybe it's their big egos or because they're control freaks—but it's a huge mistake.

I can't stress this enough; if you want to be a winner, you have to surround yourself with other winners. Your goal in life should be to look around at the company you keep and truly be able to say, "Wow, I can't believe I'm here with these great people doing this great thing!" Your business will reap the rewards if you build an amazing roster of employees who can achieve in ways one person never could.

42: LET YOUR EMPLOYEES COMPLETE YOU

The truth is, most of us mortals are nowhere close to being all-around players, so we have to compensate for our shortcomings. One way to do it is to choose your employees like an NBA owner builds a championship team. You don't draft twelve shooters, right? No, you draft a well-balanced roster that can collectively do it all.

This ties back to Lesson #12: "You can kid others but don't kid yourself." As CEO of whatever venture you're undertaking, it's up to you to be honest when you assess your strengths and weaknesses, then hire people that will complete your business and you as a businessperson.

I know you might be saying, "But Bill, I'm an all-around

player!" I like the confidence, but the odds are very good that you're not as great as you think you are! Not yet, at least.

And even if you can do it all, you're only one person. If you want to run a successful business, you have to delegate, so do it intelligently. The last thing you want to do is hire a bunch of flashy shooters that can't play together. Just look at the New York Knicks!

So are you ready to draft a perfectly balanced team of winners that will immediately make you a better CEO? Awesome! People will think you're a genius if you can build an amazing customer-first roster of employees who will buy your vision, then go out and run through walls for you.

Here are some tips for hiring and managing a killer team.

43: EMPLOYEES ARE YOUR LIFEBLOOD. MAKE THEM COUNT.

The customer may rule the business arena, but your employees are the lifeblood of your company. You can't survive without them, so don't be careless when choosing your team. Just like buying a stock or a home, you are making a serious investment when you hire somebody—so make each hire count.

Let's say I hire an employee, and I'm going to pay that person fifty grand a year, okay? I'm not looking at this employee like a $50,000 investment. I'm counting on him or her working for me for ten years, at least—so I approach this hire like it's a $500,000 investment.

Have you ever spent half a million dollars? Most of us haven't! I don't care how much money you make; half a million dollars is a big chunk of change. You have to be smart about this kind of investment.

Sure, it's easy to cut your losses if you make a bad hire, but I never hire anyone thinking, "Okay, you're hired, but I may fire you soon." I think of them as big-ticket purchases that I'm going to live with for many years.

If you can think about it like that and truly recognize that every employee you bring on is absolutely mission-critical to your success, then you will start "superchoosing" each one like you were buying your next home.

44: UNDERSTAFF AND OUTSOURCE
WHEN STARTING UP

I know a lot of you are thinking about founding your own startup, right? Stay lean and mean as long as you possibly can. That's what I've done with all my businesses, no matter how big we got. We had this inside joke at Wilmar: "Sorry, we don't have any spare vice presidents lying around!"

That was a little dig at some of our competitors who were failing because they had become too top-heavy. I've always believed allowing your business to swell with too many employees is a quick way to kill a company, yet so many companies fall into that trap.

I'm not talking about hiring too many ground troops. In today's world where everything is specialized, there is this tendency for CEOs to clog their corporate kitchen with way too many executive chefs. Who is accountable when you have multiple vice presidents who all do the same thing? Who makes the decisions?

I do things differently; I understaff and outsource. They called me "Mr. Outsource" for a reason; I outsource like crazy!

I know, I know. People have demonized outsourcing lately, and for good reason. A lot of companies are taking jobs away from Americans and sending them overseas. I get it, but not every outsourced job leaves the country! And if you're a little fish in a big pond, you can't really spend a lot of time worrying about saving the United States' economy, can you? Your first priority should be saving yourself. It's straight-up Darwinism.

It doesn't matter if it's distribution, finance, or whatever, you need to ask yourself: *How can I do it better and most cost-effectively?* My philosophy is to only roll it inside as a last resort.

But you have to be smart about outsourcing. If you screw it up, it can bite you in the butt. I know. I've had a lot of great experiences outsourcing, but I also failed at it a number of times, too. There were times when I erroneously thought I could bring a certain task outside the company, and it just didn't work out.

One example is when Wilmar was expanding and opening up new branches. When we dove into a market that didn't know us, one of our biggest assets was being able to deliver amazing customer service. In our business, this meant having a lot of trucks on the ground that could deliver goods fast—it's called route density. You don't want one delivery truck driving forty miles to drop off one box that's worth fifty bucks, right? We needed multiple trucks that all had efficient delivery routes.

I had this bright idea—why hire a bunch of full-time drivers when we could outsource the delivery jobs? How hard could it be?

Turns out, pretty hard!

As much as we gave our outsourced drivers directions, they just couldn't do it as well as our in-house guys could—and it affected our customer service. When I heard a bunch of our customers complain that they wanted one of our "real drivers," I pulled the rip cord on that experiment pretty fast.

But don't let this horror story stop you. I've also outsourced a ton of jobs that worked wonderfully. For example, right now at LendingOne, we're building the best proprietary operating system in the real estate fintech industry for the lowest cost, and we're outsourcing all our programming jobs to Russia!

Some people may ask, "How can you be a fintech company if you don't have any technology employees?" Hey, just because our tech people aren't in-house doesn't mean they aren't great employees. They do amazing work!

And times have changed. Back in my Wilmar days, we had dozens of in-house tech employees, but that was a necessity back then. Now, thanks to technology, we live in a fully connected global economy where businesses don't have to be centrally located to get the job done.

The bottom line is, I can't tell you what to roll inside and what to outsource. All I can say is to do your best not to take on any extra unnecessary weight, or all those cooks in your kitchen are going to spoil your broth—and sink your business like a lead balloon.

45: ALWAYS BE INTERVIEWING

Do you want to be a growth company? Sure you do. Who doesn't? So think like one. Here's a little tip: even if you think you already have a great team, always have something in the pipeline that allows you to meet potential new employees. Why?

You never know when you'll need to staff up.

This may sound like the opposite of the lean-and-mean philosophy (and it is, if you make a bunch of bad hires!), but I've been associated with a lot of businesses that landed a new client and suddenly were scrambling to hire good people. If you expect to be successful, always be interviewing, and be prepared to add quality employees quickly so you don't miss a beat. I'm not saying run ads and interview people every Friday, but you need to keep the mindset that you are never finished recruiting.

A good company always keeps the pipeline open.

You just never know when an employee will leave your company or stop doing great work. I can't tell you how many times I've hired a "tiger" that turned into a "toothless kitten" overnight. Sometimes, it's due to a life event, or it can be as simple as employees getting discouraged with their job. Humans are not machines. So you have to be prepared to move one if they stop producing.

I know that may sound cold, but don't be limited by the current talent on your roster. You can always get better.

Of course, you want to be loyal to your staff and have people that are loyal to you, but the reality is that 100 percent of your staff is never going to be great. And if you want to be a great company, you need to hire great people.

Loyalty will only get you so far.

46: DON'T LET LOYALTY CLOUD YOUR JUDGMENT

Here is a great example. A person I'll call Betty worked for Wilmar for twenty-seven years. A few years after I left the company, she went to work for one of our competitors that was a lot smaller. And after a while, you know what she told me?

Betty said, "Bill, you'll never believe what they do. They can have an awful employee, but because that employee's been there for years, they let them stay. They will never fire anybody."

I asked her, "Well, how are they going to become a great company that way?"

She said, "They never will."

Betty nailed it.

If you want to be great at managing employees, don't let loyalty cloud your judgment. It's a hard discipline to adopt because emotions can get involved when you work with people. They come to work for your company, and, if they do a good job, they become like family. Ideally, you want all of your employees to do a great job and rise up the corporate ladder—but what if you have great people working for you who don't have the skills to move up your ladder?

I have employed a number of people over the years who did amazing work in their existing positions—but lacked the right skill set to be promoted to management.

When they asked me, "Why am I not getting a promotion?" It was not an easy conversation to have, but I had to give it to them straight.

Think about it: what would happen if I let loyalty cloud my judgment? What if I were to say, "You know what? You've been loyal, so I'm promoting you to a manager." My underqualified employee may jump for joy initially, but guess what? We'd both lose! I would be setting that person up for failure. Not only that, the company would suffer and so would I—and that is one triple-whammy you want to avoid.

It's what they call the Peter Principle—in a hierarchy, individuals tend to be promoted to the level of their own mediocrity.

In other words, a person may be really great in the mail room, but only mediocre managing the mail room. Since typically, in most organizations, people get promotions whether they deserve them or not, suddenly you have a guy running the mail room who is only mediocre at it. He's not terrible, but he's certainly not great. Since he isn't good enough to get another promotion, he will sit there and run your mail room in a mediocre way for decades, until he retires. Why? Because he was promoted to the level of his mediocrity.

It's better not to give promotions to people who don't deserve them. Find some other way to reward them for being great at what they do, train them to move up the ladder, or cut them loose. But don't give anybody a promotion just because it seems like the friendly thing to do.

Be honest. Be empathetic. Tell your underqualified employees why you cannot promote them. Then tell them you believe in them and suggest ways they can improve their skills in order to get promoted. Give it to them straight and guess what? Your employees may not like what you have to say—but they will thank you for being honest with them and giving them a roadmap to getting a later promotion they will truly deserve.

DON'T HIRE FRIENDS

I know I may sound like a heartless guy by saying this, but don't hire your friends. If you bring friends onboard, your loyalty to your pals will inevitably cloud your judgment and come back to haunt you. Sure, I hired my friends back when I was working flea markets, but those were low-impact jobs.

They say "Don't mix business and friendship" for a reason.

Think about it: it's human nature to become emotionally invested in employees that you don't even know before you hired them. It can be doubly painful to have to fire a friend.

A great example is what happened when one of my best friends from childhood came to me after he graduated college and said, "Bill, I need to get a job. I've got another offer, but I want to work for you."

I said, "Okay, come sell for me at Wilmar. I think you'd be a great salesman."

He said, "Awesome. I'm in."

We were great pals, both single and twenty-two years old. Our parents were even friends; it was a beautiful relationship.

So he came onboard as a salesman and started building his territory. People liked him a lot. He was a good guy, very personable, but over time I realized he was a little bit on the negative side, which is counter to the attitude of most good salespeople who are usually positive by nature. I noticed he would do things like call in and talk about what he felt the company was doing wrong instead of suggesting ways we can improve how customers perceive us.

All the while, he kept saying, "I want to be a sales manager," so after he was with Wilmar for ten years, I promoted him to national sales manager.

That was a terrible mistake.

I still love the guy to death, but he just wasn't wired for the position. He couldn't manage people. He always said everything was the company's fault and nothing was the salesperson's fault.

In the end, I had to fire one of my best friends. It was a painful experience that taught me a lesson. Don't hire friends, because odds are that eventually you're going to get burned and feelings will get hurt.

47: DON'T PROMOTE TO INCOMPENTENCE

Promoting someone who was a good employee in a lesser role to incompetence is one of the worst mistakes you can make. You're killing two jobs with one bad move!

I remember when Ray came to work for me at Wilmar as a locksmith in 1992. We were still a pretty small company at the time (maybe $25 million in sales), and we decided to bring the service in-house instead of outsourcing it.

So Ray came onboard, and man, he was a tiger. He was ambitious and wanted to climb the ladder. Sure enough, a year later, there were three locksmiths working for Ray. Little by little, Ray kept getting promoted; by the time we hit $48 million in sales, Ray was the vice president of operations of the entire company.

Sounds like a success story, right?

Wrong.

I promoted him to a position that he wasn't experienced enough for. I had to let Ray go. Why? He was good at his job when we were smaller, but not so good as we grew. It took some time for me to realize this, which was my mistake.

As much as Ray probably hated my guts when I fired him back in 1999, there is a silver lining to this story. A few years after I left Wilmar, I was looking for a vice president of operations for this other company I had taken over called Aramsco.

Boom, I hired Ray back, and he did great. Why is Ray great now, when he wasn't great then? Because I hired Ray at the right time and right level this time! Being vice president of operations at Wilmar was too big for his skill set back in 1999, but being vice president of operations at Aramsco, a smaller company, was a perfect fit in 2006.

Flash-forward to today and guess what Ray is doing? He's a key executive at Aramsco! I knew Ray was a good egg. He just needed a little more experience before he was ready to move up the corporate ladder.

The lesson here is, as CEO, you can't get emotional and promote somebody you like to incompetence. You always have to do what is right for the business, while also doing your very best to try to take care of people who do good jobs for you by finding certain roles that fit them perfectly.

It's a balancing act, I know, but if you do it right, you can look back and say that you have a lot of great success stories like Ray's, where you made the right move, the employee won, and most importantly, your business won.

48: GET CREATIVE IN THE INTERVIEW PROCESS

Let's talk a little about the interview process. What's there to know, right? You just ask some questions, tell them about your company, and boom, you make a decision based on the most qualified applicant.

Wrong answer.

There are so many ways you can screw it up! The first rule of "giving good interview" is to stop talking and open your ears. I've sat in on a ton of job interviews where I watched one of my managers interview an applicant, and they don't shut up the entire time. Then after the interview is over, the applicant walks out, and the manager says to me, "Hey, I really liked that person."

I'll say, "How would you know? You did all the talking. We know nothing about this person. You told them everything about us, and all they did was shake their head and say, 'Yeah, I can do the job. How much do I get paid?'"

I'm not exaggerating when I say the majority of interviewers today do not know what the heck they're doing! They don't ask the right questions, or don't ask questions at all—and never stop talking long enough to learn anything about a person. Their entire game plan is flawed, so they never get an honest answer from anybody.

Think about the world we live in. Everyone is their own spin doctor, with their own personal brand image they want to project. Just imagine how that gets amplified in the interview process. Entire lives are airbrushed for optimal effect.

Every semi-intelligent person comes into an interview with a prepared script. They already know what the interviewer is going to say, things like "So what are your strengths?" and "What are some of your weaknesses?"

Those are the questions everyone prepares for, so why bother asking them? The pat answer is always some kind of spin that paints the applicant in some kind of ridiculously favorable light.

You'll hear answers like, "Oh, my biggest weakness is I'm a workaholic." How convenient! Your biggest weakness somehow turns out to be a strength! Hire that person! You'll never get an accurate description from someone who has a smokescreen so big, they may as well be running for office.

You have to get people to drop their fronts. How do you do that?

Get creative.

I like to ask people questions they haven't prepared for, questions that get them talking, questions like, "Tell me about your last supervisor." Most people aren't expecting that one! You can get some very revealing answers.

You may hear things like, "Oh, I don't think he's a very good guy."

And I'll ask, "Why?" Now you have them talking about somebody else and not themselves, which takes them off their talking points.

That's what you want. If you can get them speaking honestly and off the cuff, you'll learn much more about them. For instance, if you find out how a job applicant perceived his or her last boss, guess what? Odds are good that'll be the way they're going to perceive you when the job gets tough.

So throw away the blueprint for how interviews used to be done—those days are over. Approach your applicants in a way that will get them out of their "spin zone" so they are giving you an accurate read of who they really are behind their personal brand image.

49: RAID TALENT FROM OTHER COMPANIES

There is no loyalty in the capitalist jungle. You may think there is, but there isn't. If you want something or somebody, you go out and take it, and as long as you aren't breaking any laws, it's every company for themselves.

If you think you can get your best employees by raiding your competition, then don't worry about decorum. Go full Attila the Hun and pillage. I've done it. I proudly admit I've recruited guys from Wilmar to come work for my new companies. Why not? All's fair in love and war.

If a person I'm recruiting is uneasy about jumping ship, I tell them, "You think a company is going to be loyal to you if you're no longer needed? Heck no. Loyalty shouldn't flow one way."

Leverage that knowledge, and recruit, recruit, recruit. If you can find someone who can help your business that you know is being underappreciated at a competitor, release the hounds and get to poaching!

I remember there was this guy named Tony from Wilmar/Interline that I recruited to come work at Aramsco as our vice president of purchasing. It was a great position that he never would have received at Wilmar/Interline. I knew Tony wasn't growing there, so I approached him and he gladly came over. It was a win-win move that stood the test of time. Tony is still happily employed there, so it worked out great for him and the company.

Bottom line: as long as you're not breaking any laws (and there are no contracts with non-compete clauses involved), then put on your safari helmet. Happy hunting! You just never know where you're going to find undiscovered talent, so keep your eyes peeled and an open mind—and don't always judge a book by its cover.

There are diamonds in the rough everywhere. Especially now, you may find somebody who has a hobby that is actually a rare skill that your business can use. I remember this kid Tom who came to work for me at Wilmar in our customer service department when he was eighteen years old. He didn't look like he had a big upside. He didn't even have a college degree. But he was a hardworking guy, so he started out taking orders from customers over the phone.

Then one day he said to me, "Bill, I want to create programs for our computer system that will make customer service a lot better."

I asked him, "Tom, how do you know about computers outside of turning one on?"

He said, "I've taught myself how to program ever since I was twelve years old."

I said, "Tom, calm down. We have a company that does this for us!"

But Tom kept persisting, and it turned out the kid was an amazing programmer. I gave him a chance to do something different, and he knocked it out of the park.

Once I realized I had this brilliant guy on my hands toiling away in the customer service department, I promoted him to director of management information systems, and he did a great job.

I used to call him Stevie Wonder because I'd walk into his office and he'd be sitting at his keyboard with his eyes closed, typing away. I'd ask, "Hey, Tom, what are you doing?"

And he'd say, "I'm programming."

I'd say, "But your eyes are shut."

And he'd say, "I know it. I see it better this way."

Did I raid him, too?

Oh, yeah, he's vice president of information technology at Aramsco now!

50: NO RAISES? C'MON!

I hear this all the time: "We can't give this employee a raise because he or she already makes too much money."

What kind of logic is that? Then that person shouldn't be working here.

Don't punish employees who negotiated a nice salary just because you're experiencing slight buyer's remorse. If this person is hitting their performance measurements and doing a good job, he or she should get a raise. At the very minimum, give them a cost-of-living raise—as far as I'm concerned, everybody deserves that. Now if this person is not doing a good job, then it's time to cut your losses, but I've noticed most managers will do anything not to fire someone.

What I normally hear is, "Oh, we don't want to fire the person. Instead, we're just not going to give them any raises." Seriously? C'mon, you're being a wimp. Suck it up, and make a decision!

My philosophy is never to settle for overpriced talent when you know you can do better. This kind of inaction is how bloated rosters lead to stagnant organizations that die because they are too afraid to change.

Once you've done your due diligence and the writing is on the wall, it's time to tighten your belt and sharpen your axe already, for the sake of the company.

MANAGING IS NOT A FOUR-LETTER WORD

Now that you have superchosen a balanced roster of employees that will help turn your business into a global force, don't take your foot off the gas. You can't just drop them off at their first day of school and expect them to be perfect. You have to take an active role in their progress. There will be an acclimation period for virtually everyone, but if you hired the right people, they should start performing pretty fast.

If not? You can't fire a bad employee fast enough.

But more on that later. Let's not focus on the negative stuff first. Most of your new hires are going to be great, but they have to be managed.

51: MANAGING IS LIKE PARENTING

If you don't have children, you may not get this, but managing employees is a lot like parenting. I'm not being condescending, but if you're a parent, you will understand the analogy. If you ask your kids to do something, do you assume they'll do it? No way. You have to follow up and make sure they do it right.

You're going to have to manage your employee developmental process exactly the same way. It's never as simple as just saying,

"Okay, David, you're hired. Do what I tell you, and things will be great." You have to refine your working relationship with your people as you go along. There is no blueprint for success, but you have to find out how to communicate with and motivate each individual. You have to know when a certain employee needs to be coddled or when an employee responds to a (figurative) kick in the pants.

I can't tell you how to read people (that's a different book entirely), so I won't spend a lot of time on this subject, but just know this: a huge part of being a good manager is understanding what buttons to push to get the most out of your employees. Push the wrong buttons, and it doesn't matter how talented the employee is. It's like driving a Ferrari in reverse with the emergency brake on. A total waste of resources!

52: PEOPLE DO WHAT'S INSPECTED RATHER THAN WHAT'S EXPECTED

You can't expect every employee is going to be a self-starter who does awesome work on his or her own. Sure, it would be great if life operated on that principle, but that's not reality. Your employees need you to watch out for them.

Here's a good rule to manage by: people do what's inspected of them, not what's expected of them. What does that mean? If you leave your employees' success up to the expectations you have for them, you're going to be sorely disappointed every time. You have to instill quality-control practices into everything you do, and that goes for managing your employees.

You have to train them—then check in with them frequently to make sure they're doing a great job. You have to stay on top of them until you can trust them to do the job themselves, and then you still need to check up on them!

Sometimes people say, "But Bill, it's expensive to train people, and then they'll just leave and take another job eventually anyway!"

My response is what they teach at Disney—it's better to train people and have them eventually leave than not train them and have them stay!

I know I may sound like a micromanager. The word has an ugly connotation these days. No one wants to be known as that kind of boss, but the most famous geniuses the world has ever known were total micromanagers! Do you think Leonardo Da Vinci or Michelangelo trusted their assistants to pick the right color of paint for their masterpieces?

I'm not saying I am a genius or that you should be a micromanager. All I'm saying is, don't confuse micromanaging with actual managing. You have to strike the right balance between autonomy and control to get it right. Let me give you a great example.

At LendingOne, we built this awesome proprietary algorithm that funnels our leads to the right salesperson based on lead type, geography, and score. I was dinking around the system one day, and I noticed there were a lot of incomplete applications from customers just sitting there in queues. No one had touched them! When I saw this, I said to myself, "If we have their contact information, shouldn't someone be following up with these people?"

Just because customers created an incomplete application doesn't mean they don't need help, right? There are a million reasons why a person might not be able to complete an application. Maybe they don't know how to fill it out, or they get interrupted and have to log out. At the very minimum, you know these people are interested because they started to fill out an application, right?

So I walked over to my sales manager, Rich, and casually asked, "Did you know we have a ton of leads in the system that have not been followed up on?"

Rich said, "What are you talking about?"

And I said, "Are you going into the system to see what's going on?"

And Rich said, "I'm not a micromanager."

I thought, *Really? It looks like you're not even managing.*

Was Rich afraid of being considered a micromanager, or was he just being lazy? Personally, I think he was using micromanaging as an excuse. When I pointed this out to Rich, he said he "couldn't fathom that some of our salespeople weren't following up on leads," which gave me serious doubts about his management skills.

I eventually would have to fire the guy, but on this day, I took matters into my own hands and did Rich's job for him. I found out what queue the incomplete apps were in, and I emailed the guys who were in charge. I said, "Hey, guys, how are you? Will you do me a favor and check out all the incomplete apps in the queue and see if you can follow up on them?"

I was really cool about it. I never put anybody on the spot. I didn't have to. Sending that email was all it took to get the results I wanted. Those salespeople knew I was watching them, so they had to get working. And they did. I guarantee if I log into the LendingOne system right now, there will not be one untouched lead that's more than an hour old.

See how even the hint of inspection gets people to do their jobs? That's why I'm a big fan of spot-checking people's work, especially the departments that have direct client interface.

Back in the Wilmar days, we had a certain protocol for how a box was supposed to be packed with merchandise, so every once in a while, we'd have spot inspections and open up a box that had already been taped up to make sure it was properly packed.

You'd better believe we were able to catch some less-than-perfect work before it reached the customer! Can you imagine if we never thought about that kind of thing and had to wait for customers to call in and say, "Look at the way I got this stuff delivered!"

I never wanted that to happen, so that is why I instilled quality-control steps at every level of every organization I've ever been a part of. You would be wise to do the same thing. Just knowing that their output may be inspected goes a long way toward making sure your team members are doing excellent work at all times.

53: MANAGEMENT BY WALKING AROUND

I'm a people person. I like to get out and mix with my employees. It's just part of who I am. I sincerely enjoy it, but it's not just a social habit. It can also be a tactical move. Remember how I handed out WIT (Whatever It Takes) buttons to my customer service team? Well, I have another acronym that I'm a big believer in called MBWA (Management by Walking Around). I don't hand out MBWA buttons, but I've got to tell you, I think it's a hugely underrated management skill.

The idea is, to be a successful CEO, you can't position yourself as some faceless leader who sits in your ivory tower and orders people around. That doesn't humanize you to anybody, much less your team, whom you want to inspire. Don't be the kind of boss who has your own personal espresso maker in your office! Go out and get your coffee at the coffee machine in the employee kitchen like everybody else. Be a populist leader. If you get out of your office and mix with your people, a couple things will happen.

The most important thing is, your employees will know you're visible and that you are one of them. The second thing getting out there does is that it allows you to get to know your people, their families, and their interests. You can run into them and chitchat about life. Ask them things like, "Hey, Suzie, how're you doing? How was Johnny's soccer game?" Forget the business side of your relationship for a minute, and show them that you care about them as humans, not just as cogs in the machine.

Don't be phony about it. You have to be sincere, because the fakers will be exposed. You don't want to come off as some guy who is making his monthly walk around the office like an egomaniacal dictator of a nation. Everybody jokes about that kind of guy on Facebook.

It has to be real. You want your employees to think you're just walking around, but really you are conducting MBWA. There is no alternative. If you don't do MBWA in some way, your people won't buy your leadership or run through walls for you. In fact, they may run out the door to one of your competitors that knows how to treat their people like human beings, not robotic drones.

54: CUT DOWN ON MEETINGS

I mentioned this earlier, but I don't understand the obsession with hour-long meetings in our culture. Don't people have better things to do with their day? In these go-go modern times, why not have action-packed, ten-minute meetings? Cut the small talk and the bagels and lox. Get in, get out, and move on! This is not a new concept; a lot of successful CEOs are already doing it—but not enough, if you ask me.

It's not just the length of meetings that bothers me; it's the frequency. There are way too many companies that have meetings on top of meetings to the point of absurdity. How is any work being done if your day is booked up? While all these companies are in back-to-back all-day meetings, their competition is eating their lunch.

Don't waste time with too many meetings, especially during prime business hours. This is something you can instill into the core of your company culture. Train your employees to cut the small talk in meetings and refrain from equivocating every issue on the agenda. What is the point of going around the room to find out everyone's feelings on an issue? Most business decisions are not made by a collective, so why pretend that's the way things work? It's not only a huge waste of time, but it also breeds a culture of indecision.

Meet long enough to cover the important items, then keep moving with the rest of your day. Your burgeoning startup will be the better for it when your employees are doing their jobs instead of sitting around talking about doing them over coffee and donuts!

55: GET OUT OF YOUR COMFORT ZONE AND DELEGATE

I know I told you to do WIT (Whatever It Takes) to succeed—but that doesn't mean you should try to do everything yourself. Sure, it's a great philosophy when you're in startup mode, but if the team you built starts kicking butt and becomes a perennial powerhouse, you don't have to keep carrying the team.

I know it's hard to do if you're used to scoring fifty points a game, but you need to learn to trust your teammates and delegate. Think about when Michael Jordan or LeBron James started winning titles. They didn't keep scoring sixty points a game; they made their teammates better. They played better defense. They got their teammates involved and maximized the talent on the entire roster.

The same thing goes in the business world. It took me years to take this lesson to heart. Back when I was starting Wilmar, I tried to do it all for way too long. Then one day, I realized I could better serve the company if I maximized my time and didn't try to be everywhere and do everything.

You could say I was a control freak, but I had to be a control freak to succeed when I was bootstrapping my first startup. I never felt like it was a burden to dive in and understand how every aspect of our business worked; I loved doing it! But that kind of thinking can only last so long. You can't get stuck in your old ways, even when those old ways are working. It may sound counterintuitive, but doing too much can hurt your company.

This is one skill they don't teach you at CEO boot camp: learn to let it go.

You've just hired an amazing team, right? Then trust your instincts, and let your employees do the jobs that you hired them to do. I finally learned to delegate ten years after I started my first company! I wouldn't say I'm totally hands-off now, but once I train new employees, I let them do their thing. I tell them, "Call me if you need me, and keep me up to speed. Just don't surprise me with bad news after the fact when I can't help you do something about it."

How did I stop sweating everything and learn to delegate? It all started back in 1987. Marty, my dad, was already phasing out of the day-to-day operations of the company. I was the president but still doing a lot of the purchasing and sales. I had stayed lean and mean as long as I could, but in '87, we finally got so big that I had to break down and hire my first executive.

His name was Abby Greene (no relation). He was the first guy I hired that had corporate management experience; he'd worked for big corporations like PepsiCo. While Abby was with us, he had a lot of influence on me. He was the guy who finally convinced me to trust my team and delegate. I remember shortly after I hired him, he came into my office and saw my desk covered with all these boxes full of parts.

Abby took one look at my setup and asked, "What are you doing?"

"I'm working on the purchasing orders for the plumbing specialty parts," I said.

"Why are you doing that?"

"I've got to do it. You know, Abby, this is pretty technical stuff."

Abby shuts the door and says, "Bill, can I talk to you? With all due respect, you want to know what's going on here?"

I said, "What's going on, Abby? I'm busy. Can you make it fast?"

He said, "You're doing all this because you're afraid of doing what you really need to do."

I looked up at him and said, "What do I really need to be doing?"

"Be the president of the company," he said. "You're in your comfort zone doing the purchasing, when you need to be out there leading the people and driving this company. What if you delegate all this to someone? What's the worst that can happen? Maybe that person is going to make a few mistakes that you didn't make. So what?"

Abby's advice hit me like a bolt of lightning. It's not like I wasn't leading the company—but he was spot-on with his assessment. I said, "You know, Abby, you're right. Thanks for the tip." Then I grabbed all the boxes on my desk, walked down the hall, and dropped them on the desk of one of my employees. I said, "Tony, it's yours now. Let me know if you need me."

The moral of this story is that the old adage "Don't fix what isn't broken" does not apply to a growing business. In fact, I like to say, "If it ain't broken, fix it anyway."

I've told this story to a lot of young entrepreneurs over the years, and it always hits home with them. Just because you're having success and everyone is comfortable with what they're doing, don't think that it can't be done better.

It can be done better. It has to.

56: ENCOURAGE EMPLOYEES TO ADMIT WHEN THEY DON'T KNOW

I've been managing people for nearly forty years, and I've found a lot of employees are afraid to admit when they screwed up, because they had strict parents or are used to working for bosses who hammer them for making a mistake.

That's not the way I operate. Not at all.

I encourage my team to admit when they are wrong.

How do I do this? I admit when I'm wrong.

If I screw something up, I stand up, take the bullet, and let them know that I'm going to do it better next time. Of course, it's easy for CEOs to do this, because who is going to take us to task (except the shareholders if you're a public company)?

So it's not a big deal for me, but admitting that you screwed up is really touchy for some people. Even saying, "I don't know" is hard for some employees. Knowing all this, I advise you to make a concerted effort to encourage your employees to speak the truth at all times. Think about it. What is more productive, for employees to admit they don't know or for them to mislead you into thinking they have it handled? The truth is always the best way to approach any situation, so do it head-on with the facts and cut away all the CYA (cover your ass) BS.

I like to tell my team, "It's not a stupid question if you don't know the answer. So let's think about a solution as a team." And look, everybody makes mistakes, right? So, if you foster an environment where your employees are brutally afraid to admit they made an error, they're going to try to "cover it up," which is going to cost you way more than the initial error.

Let your employees know that it's okay to speak the truth. If you can get that across, it will create a healthy problem-solving environment in your company that is built on honesty and trust.

57: YOU CAN'T MEASURE TRUST AND LOYALTY

Speaking of honesty and trust, is it possible to measure loyalty and trust in your employees? It's a great question. I'll let you know when I figure it out.

The fact is, you can't expect complete loyalty from your employees. Everybody wants to better themselves. It's the American way to move up the ladder. If there is a better opportunity at another company, they should take it. Like I said when I talked about raiding other companies for talent, there is no loyalty in love and war!

If an employee is making $60,000 a year and gets a job offer for $80,000 at another company, he or she has to take that job, and that's fine with me. Of course, it would be great if you had employees who would give you a heads-up, walk into your office, and say, "I love working here, but I need a raise or I'm going to have to start looking for a job." It would also be great if a valued employee gave you a chance to counter if he or she received another offer. Sometimes, that happens. But other times, employees will just come in and resign. And I can't fault them for that.

So don't waste your time trying to predict who will stay and who will go. It's impossible to tell (probably. Like I said, I'm still working on it).

I will say I feel comfortable hiring people I already trust. These people aren't friends, and I'm not doing anybody any favors by hiring them. However, they are trusted commodities that I know have a good track record of reliability.

Here is a good example of what I mean. At LendingOne, I hired a guy named Matt Neisser as my chief operating officer. I met him when he was working with my good friend Fred Berlinsky, who I partnered with on a number of commercial real estate investments. I was able to vet Matt personally over an eight-year time frame. He impressed me so much, I started asking him to sit in on a couple of board of directors conference calls with me. After he left Fred to look for a private equity job in New York, I hired him to help me launch LendingOne. It was a no-brainer decision that has worked out great.

Do your best to hire people with strong character. You can check references and vet the heck out of applicants during the interview process, but at some point, you are going to have to trust your gut and follow your instincts.

Your gut has gotten you this far. Why stop now?

58: YOU CAN'T FIRE BAD HIRES FAST ENOUGH

If you make a mistake and hire a person that you know is not going to make it, cut your losses and get rid of him or her as quickly as possible. Don't let a bad apple linger and hope and pray things are going to get better. They're not! It is only going to get worse if you let the cancer spread throughout your team; it will affect your business and may even infect the rest of your employees.

That's why I like to tell my new hires that they're working with a sixty- or ninety-day introductory period. I say, "Let's see how it goes before we commit." It's like dating a new hire instead of marrying him or her immediately. Why get the law involved if you're not sure?

A good manager will know in a few weeks if the new hire is a good employee, so I highly recommend the introductory period. It allows you to avoid a lot of legal issues that may go with having to terminate a contract early.

And don't get me started on the huge mess that can come if you have a disgruntled employee who feels they have been wrongly terminated. They can become vindictive, so nip those issues in the bud and move on.

59: TRAIN, TRAIN, TRAIN!

Now that you've got your awesome team assembled and you've trained them and trust them to do their jobs—I hate to break it to you, but the training is never over. It is not a one-time event. You have to keep developing all your employees as your business evolves, forevermore.

Just because you put employees through a two-week training period doesn't mean you can forget about them. No way. You've got to follow that up with another training session three months later . . . then another one after that . . . and then another one. You get the idea: train, train, refresh, and train some more. You can't get stale: you have to keep on top of it.

I highly suggest that you hire someone to run your training and development programs from your company's inception. It doesn't matter how small you are—do it now. Don't wait until you've got a hundred employees.

Remember: it's much easier to make incremental changes to your company culture than large ones. You can do this by slightly improving your processes and then training your employees on the changes as you go along.

This is at the very heart of why I'm a huge fan of continued education. My philosophy on it is simple:

Your team is never complete.

Every employee is always a work in progress, including yourself.

It can always be done better. It has to be if you want to win a title. And who doesn't want to win a championship ring?

60: AVOID PARALYSIS BY ANALYSIS

Over the years, I have encountered a lot of managers, directors, vice presidents, and (even) C-level executives who have a hard time "pulling the trigger" on a decision. Some might call these "nervous Nellies" careful leaders, but (if you ask me) I think these people just lacked the confidence to put themselves out there and make a decision.

This is how a "culture of indecision" spreads like wildfire throughout a company. If employees see their boss can't make a decision, what lesson do you think they are going to take away from that? It's not a positive one, I can tell you that!

As the CEO of your company, you can't get caught up in "paralysis by analysis." If you are stuck on a decision, ask yourself, "What's the worst thing that can happen if I make the wrong move?" No matter what you choose, it can't be as bad as what happens when you stay paralyzed, which is nothing!

If I could instill any one trait into your hard drive, it would be to believe in your decision-making ability and to have a sense of urgency that won't let you procrastinate another day. Passing the buck is death in the business world! If you are waffling on a decision, guess who isn't? Your competition, that's who.

So take some ownership of the moment, and your employees will respect and then follow your lead. Whenever you are confronted with a decision, ask yourself: What good is "passing the buck" going to do for your business? Remember, nothing is perfect in life, and neither are you—so forget about perfection and make the damn decision already.

The bottom line on people? Don't buy into the mantra a lot of cynical businesspeople live by—that "it's impossible to find good people." It's possible to find great people! But you've got to have the right mindset, you've got to be able to trust and delegate, and you've also got to be able to make the hard decisions when they arise. Otherwise, you'll be doing a disservice to your employee, his or her fellow employees, the company as a whole, and yourself.

KEY TAKEAWAYS

- Surround yourself with people who will give you the good and the bad news.
- Don't be the smartest person in the room—fill the room with smart people.
- Balance your team with people who bring varied skills to your business.
- Approach each potential hire like a long-term investment, but don't over hire in the beginning—be willing to outsource when necessary.
- Loyalty does not equal performance, nor does it equal automatic promotions. Be honest with employees about how they can earn promotions.
- Maintain a presence by walking the floor, and reduce meeting times.
- Friendship and business rarely work well together. Do not hire your pals. You'll regret it later on.

CHAPTER 7

CRUSHING IT IN SALES

There are no traffic jams along the extra mile.

—Roger Staubach

LET'S TAKE INVENTORY. Are you becoming comfortable making strategic hiring decisions? Are you totally engaged in your business from every angle? Are you mustering the drive to give your company all the resources it needs to overcome cutthroat competition? Great! Because once you've got all those components in place, it's time to start selling. How, exactly? I wouldn't say it's an exact science, but after decades of starting and maintaining successful businesses, I know what it takes to crush your competition through smart, targeted sales techniques. In this chapter, we'll cover exactly what kind of salespeople you want working for you, as well as different kinds of sales tactics that will help you succeed.

61: NO HARVEST WITHOUT RAINMAKERS

In the last chapter, we talked about how to hire, train, and manage employees, but I want to go deeper to discuss the vital importance of your sales and marketing team to your future success. It doesn't matter how great the product or service you are selling is, if you want your business to be the best, you need to hire some "rainmakers" to help get you there.

What if you are the primary rainmaker at your company? That's great. So was I for many of my Wilmar years, but in large-scale business, one person can't "conjure rain" alone. One "medicine man" might have done it on the Kansas plains in the 1800s, but to max out your potential in the world of commerce, you have to hire a take-no-prisoners group of extremely persuasive people who will sell your business to the outside world.

Some people think sales can be taught. Can it really?

I believe it most definitely can, but after nearly forty years in the game, I have a sneaking suspicion you have to be born with the right type of personality to be an absolutely amazing salesperson. But I'm ready for one of you readers—if you think you were born without the sales DNA, but are a phenomenal salesperson—to prove me wrong on that one!

A GREAT SALESPERSON SHOULD BE . . .

Let me tell you, people ask me all the time, "What makes a good salesperson?" They think I should know a little something about it since I've been selling stuff since kindergarten!

I guess I'm pretty okay at sales. I never had a problem selling because I always believed in the products I sold. Repeat after me: Sales is not an exact science, nor is it an art form. Being a great salesperson has everything to do with resilience, willpower, persistence, smarts, and charisma.

This may sound crazy, but I think I can kind of tell who is going to be a good salesperson after just talking with him or her for a few minutes. You get this feeling just being around that person. Here's a little tip: you feel enthused after talking to the great ones.

There is definitely a certain type I'm looking for when I'm hiring sales staff. Would you like to see my list of prerequisites?

Here are some of the telltale traits I look for in a sales rep.

By the way, if you ever interview for a sales job at LendingOne, now you have a cheat sheet.

THE TELLTALE TRAITS OF A GREAT SALESPERSON

1. A great salesperson has to be high-energy and self-confident.
2. A great salesperson has to be hungry to eat (i.e., earn money).
3. A great salesperson must be extremely knowledgeable about his or her work.
4. A great salesperson knows how to push people's buttons and understands how to respond to every customer request.
5. A great salesperson sees obstacles as a challenge.

A big misconception is that sales is only about hitting your numbers. Not true! There's a lot more that goes into the job, but I've found that for some reason, some sales reps today don't understand this. These reps are all about their numbers, like pure shooters in basketball. I'm a pure shooter myself, so you would think I could appreciate this type of single-minded salesperson. But I can't say that I do. You know why?

One-dimensional shooters are a dime a dozen.

Sure, they can hit their shots, but they have no other skills. What happens if their shot is off? If they aren't banging calls and closing deals, they are practically useless.

THE INTANGIBLES ARE HUGE

I'm not going to sit here and tell you hitting your numbers isn't extremely important—it is—but there is a lot more to being a great salesperson than just draining shots. What do I mean? I'm talking about all the intangibles that go into the job.

All that other stuff is not always sexy, but it's what separates the great ones from the merely good. I've personally hired hundreds of sales reps who could "get them to sign on the line that is dotted," to quote Alec Baldwin in *Glengarry Glen Ross* (one of the best movies ever about sales). But what about maintaining the client relationship and providing great service to your customers after you close the sale?

Remember, nothing ever goes perfectly in life, especially in business, so it is vital that you have sales reps who will get on the phone and ease your clients' minds when someone (God forbid) screws up.

Sales is not just about bagging the elephant! You have to learn to feed and care for it too. The "pure shooter" salespeople overlook the importance of client maintenance. They think that part of the job is beneath them. They just want to bang calls and stuff their commission with more bucks.

This is a big philosophical mistake . . . huge.

62: ALWAYS BE SINCERE

To be a great salesperson, you have to truly want to serve your clients through the entire customer experience. You have to care so much about them that you will find a way to solve their problems, long after the commission has hit your account.

I have had to fire a lot of "one-tool" sales reps that didn't get this. They just didn't have the intangibles necessary to be great. Even to this day, I can tell when a sales rep is not doing the intangibles simply by observing that person's body language at work.

When "bad apples" are presented with servicing an existing customer and I see them complaining about it instead of slapping on a WIT pin and doing whatever it takes to get the job done— it's a big red flag. I know the bad apple won't stay around long.

You have to be sincerely invested in making your customers happy, even when you aren't being paid a dime to show it. That is, if you want to be one of the greats.

I know what you're asking, "How can you train someone to become a great salesperson?" I'm not some legendary sales guru like Dale Carnegie or David Ogilvy, but if you ask me, the first step is to train people to be themselves. Let me preface that by saying, I hope you aren't a horrible person. If you are, forget what I said. Don't be yourself. Be a good person!

Look like one, and act like one. Be sincere.

If you can pull this off, I'm telling you, you will already be so far ahead of the pack. What do I mean? There is something about sales that attracts phonies. Think used car salesman. Sales has become a four-letter word in some households, and rightly so. The entire industry today is overrun with legions of insincere hucksters who would sell their grandmothers for a cup of water in the desert.

The last thing you want to do is hire a sales rep who isn't authentic. Any hint of phoniness is going to turn off clients. That's why used car salesmen have become a punchline.

How do you convey sincerity to clients?

You can't fake it.

You really have to believe that your company makes the "best stuff" to sell that belief to your clients. Remember, no one buys anything from somebody they don't trust.

Take my good friend Ralph. He's an awesome salesman who started with Wilmar back in 1980, and believe it or not, is still with them today. What makes Ralph so special? He's a consistent and persistent salesman who believes in the value of his company and also cares about his customers. His sincerity bleeds into everything he does, so you can trust the guy, and he never lets you down. I've known Ralph for thirty-six years, and when he says he's going to do something, he does it! To use Miguel Ruiz's phrase, Ralph is "impeccable with his word," which is huge in the sales game.

63: ENGAGE WITH THE CUSTOMER!

If you asked Ralph, he would tell you that much of selling comes down to finding a way to personally connect with a customer. My dad gave me one of the most important sales lessons I ever learned: If you want customers to love you, engage them on a personal level before you talk business.

This seems like a no-brainer, right? Well, it's not.

It's amazing how many sales calls I've witnessed where the salesperson doesn't engage the customer first. How hard is this to do? It's as simple as asking, "How are you?" or "Did you have a nice weekend?" This kind of small talk can't be scripted, so don't be a phony about it. Be sincere! It has to occur naturally (per the situation) for it to be effective.

Okay, let's say you are starting a conversation with someone you don't know very well. But one thing you do know is they are from Dallas, Texas, right? So before you start talking business, how about breaking the ice by saying something like, "Think the Cowboys are going to finally do it this year?"

You will be amazed how fast their guards go down if you do it right.

The same goes for when you are wrapping up a meeting. Let's say, in this case, you know the client fairly well and have met with him or her a number of times. You might be comfortable enough to say something like, "Any plans for the weekend?"

I'm telling you, it's amazing how one little verbal cue will get people talking about their family, kids, or a specific interest.

Now, if you can take it a step further and file away the personal information they share with you—and bring it back up in a subsequent meeting? That kind of follow-up will show your customers how much you care about them!

Clearly, this lesson applies to more than just sales, but so many people don't understand its importance in sales success. Engage customers on a personal level, and treat them like they're special if you want them to treat you specially, too.

64: THE CUSTOMER ALWAYS COMES FIRST

Great sales reps have to be two things at once; they have to be fast-moving problem-solvers for their customers, and ruthless rainmakers for their business. If it sounds like sales reps have got two mouths to feed, it's because they do.

How can a sales rep serve both the customer and the business without doing a disservice to one or both?

Do I have to answer this for you?

The customer is always right; they always come first!

I'm not saying to give your product or service away for free; we all have to make money. But don't oversell people on stuff they don't need just to make it rain. If your sales reps are looking out for their customers every step of the way, you will never go wrong in the eyes of your clients, and guess what?

The customers' opinion is what matters the most.

HUNTERS VERSUS FARMERS

Did you know sales reps almost always fall into one of two categories? It's true. You will find both of these sales archetypes in virtually every sales organization. There are hunters and there are farmers.

Hunters tend to be aggressive ball hawks that are always looking to score. They can be overbearing if they aren't careful. Hunters don't want to deal with minutiae, but they never have a problem shooting the ball—that is, asking for the order. They're great at hunting sales commissions, because they are only looking out for themselves, not their customers. Customers can smell this kind of phoniness from a mile away.

At the other end of the spectrum are the farmers, who are great at maintaining customer relationships and fixing things when they go wrong—but are not good at going for the jugular. They faint at the sight of blood; when it's crunch time, they shy away from asking for the order!

Both of these approaches are inherently flawed.

There are plenty of good sales reps who are super at doing one thing, either hunting or farming, but very few who can do both extremely well, which is unfortunate because a great salesperson should strike a perfect balance between the two. They have to sincerely care about clients, while also filling up the stat sheet for their employer.

Believe me, being outstanding at both is easier said than done.

What if you happen to discover a salesperson that is a hunter and a farmer? Let me tell you, hold on to that employee, because he or she is worth a mint!

65: ASK FOR THE ORDER!

I want to drive this point home. In life, "ask, and you shall receive."

It's so true. I see so many salespeople who are doing everything well, except one thing, and that's asking for the order. How hard is it to ask, "Would you like me to order this for you today?" For some shy types, it can be the hardest thing in the world.

It's unbelievable, but a lot of so-called salespeople don't know how to ask for the order. It is Salesmanship 101, plain and simple. The number one rule is, "Don't forget to ask for the order."

You'd think this would be a given with salespeople, but it's not. I still see it all the time. It drives me nuts when I observe one of my sales reps, who is confident and knowledgeable about the company's offerings, still forget his or her most important duty. If you can't ask for the order, you need to hit the showers, get off the court, and let someone else shoot the ball.

There is no scoring without shooting. So shoot the ball already!

66: I REPEAT: BE PERSISTENT AND CONSISTENT

This lesson never gets old. It really does apply to everything in life, but especially sales, which is often a war of attrition. It takes time to see results. You will get the door slammed in your face—but you have to keep coming back and knocking on that door repeatedly, if you want to get results.

You have to be consistently persistent to get anywhere in this world. I just told one of my sales reps a few days ago, "If the client doesn't call you back in forty-eight hours, you've got to call again."

I must have given that order a zillion times in my life!

Persistency and consistency always win out, even if you are selling to one of your regular customers. That's how you create raving fans of your work, by showing your regular clients you care about them so much that you are on top of everything. As for how to deal with a potential customer who doesn't pull the trigger on a sale, don't give up on that client.

Make sure that customer knows you will be calling again. Be clear, and say exactly when you will be stopping by the customer's office to revisit your conversation. Never let up. I'm telling you—it will pay off!

Too many salespeople these days don't understand that being consistent and persistent is a major part of their job. You have to teach them the ropes. You have to stay on top of your sales reps so they stay on top of their customers. Drill it into their brains that, unless they are persistent in life, it's going to be hard to succeed at anything, especially sales.

67: WHAT'S LUCK GOT TO DO WITH IT?

Let me be crystal clear on this one: closing a sale has nothing to do with luck. Reps that can't close like to blame their failures on bad luck, but that's just an excuse. Luck happens when preparation meets opportunity, which means you're the only one who can put yourself in a position to be lucky.

How can you help luck along? Try doing a little more homework than your competitors, arriving early for a meeting, or attending one of your client's kid's soccer games. Deals can be made anytime and anywhere, so you have to be prepared to strike when the opportunity presents itself. It may take time, but if you have placed yourself for the opportunity, it will most likely come.

I probably have hundreds of examples where I put myself in a position to be lucky, but here is a good one where I followed my gut and it really paid off.

Back in 1990, I joined an organization called the National Multifamily Housing Council (NMHC). It was a small group at the time, around forty to fifty members, mostly senior executives and the owners of apartment buildings, who met to discuss the apartment industry, network, and hear a few speakers.

I noticed after I joined that a lot of the senior executives who attended this event were not the day-to-day decision makers at their company. They delegated all the stuff that related to my business, like purchasing maintenance supplies.

I remember other people I knew asked me, "Why did you join that organization? What a waste of money and time."

I said, "Look. You never know who's going to take an interest in you."

I kept going to the meetings. I admit I was kind of intimidated. I didn't know anybody in the group. I was still a young man; I had a decent-sized company but no formal education like everyone else in the room. I didn't have the confidence I have today, but I kept going anyway. I would attend their cocktail parties in Washington, DC, and stand around feeling awkward. Yeah, I'd talk to a few people, but the entire experience was agonizing!

I was not having any fun, but I kept at it for years.

Then the crowd for the event started getting bigger and kept getting bigger every year, which was encouraging. It got to be so large, I eventually made some valuable friends. It took me years, but some of the "non-decision-making executives" connected me with the folks in their organizations who did make the supply purchasing decisions. Do you know how valuable those head honcho introductions were for me? They were priceless!

Want to know the best part of the story?

The minute Wilmar went public, everyone in the group who didn't care about getting to know me or Wilmar suddenly was interested in me. You know the old saying, "People like to be around successful people?" Well, it's true. Everybody wanted to be my friend after we went public. Before that? I was a wallflower that most everyone ignored! But the year Wilmar went public, you'd have thought I was close pals with everybody in the organization.

Can you see what I did here?

I put myself in a position to be lucky by joining an organization where I could get noticed by influencers in my industry. It was a painful experience for years, but when it paid off, it really paid off.

Meanwhile, none of Wilmar's competitors were putting themselves in the same position to succeed. I was way out in front of everybody else on this one—and that is where you have to be if you want to succeed in sales.

Luck has nothing to do with it.

68: THE COMPANY OWNS THE CUSTOMER

It doesn't matter what business you're in, you are inevitably going to hire a salesperson or two whose egos are so big, they think they have the magic touch when it comes to signing clients. They think every sale they make is based on their special relationship with the customer.

Pardon my French, but that is total BS.

The company owns the customer. You should never get a client because he or she has a personal relationship with one of your salespeople. You should win their business because you have a great company that provides amazing products and services!

Yes, there are some situations where you may want to hire a sales rep with a good book of clients, but don't make a habit of it. Trust me, you want as little of your business as possible based on personal relationships with your sales reps.

How can you make sure your clients are loyal to your business, not to one of your sales reps? As CEO, it's your job to make sure your customers have formed an emotional (and hopefully, unbreakable) bond with your products or services.

To do this, your customers need to know everything about you and your business. You have to sell them on your value so they keep coming back. The last thing you want is for customers to keep coming back just because they have a one-off relationship with one of your sales reps. Why, you ask?

What happens if that salesperson leaves? The sales rep could take his or her book of clients to another company!

Even though I always have my sales teams sign non-compete agreements, which is standard, I also work really hard to make sure all of my customers are sticky to the company and not to a single relationship.

POACHING IS NOT ALLOWED

Never let an ex-employee poach your clients. You have to build a strong foundation of trust to make every customer relationship stick. If you can't find a way to form that bond of trust with your clients, and their favorite sales rep leaves, you can kiss your relationship goodbye!

When one of my Wilmar sales reps left to work for a competitor, it didn't work out very well for that person. Why? The company owned the customer! When we lost a salesperson, we retained 80 percent of his or her book of business.

How did we do it?

We serviced the heck out of those customers so they knew Wilmar had their backs. We didn't just focus on establishing relationships with one contact person in a customer's network; we made a point to sell Wilmar's story throughout the customer's entire organization (more on that next). That way, when one of our sales reps moved to another company, we could retain most of his or her client book because we had installed customer retention support practices at the corporate level.

I strongly suggest you instill the same customer retention practices in your business. It really has to come from the top down if you want to make it a priority, so make it a priority. I'm already instilling best practices that will ensure every customer stays with LendingOne, even if their favorite sales rep walks out the door.

How am I ensuring this happens?

I'm making sure LendingOne has amazing customer service at every touchpoint. I'm not just talking about the sales team. I mean everyone. That, my friends, is how you retain clients. By being awesome at everything. And it's working, so far!

Remember how I had to terminate Rich, our sales manager? You may be curious to know what happened to his book of business when I let him go. Well, I'm happy to report we retained 90 percent of his business, because his customers loved dealing with LendingOne.

That is why I'm so passionate about providing the best customer service on earth. It helps you retain clients, even when rock-star sales reps jump ship and try to take their book with them!

69: SELL THROUGH THE ORGANIZATION

You have to learn to sell through an entire organization. Spread the love around! Why focus your sales skills on just one person when there is an entire organization to impress? You will want to have as many people as possible on your side if you want to keep a business customer in the long term.

Here is a good example of what I mean from my Wilmar days. Quite a few of our apartment building customers were managed or owned by larger regional or national companies. There was a pecking order when it came to who made the buying decisions in these companies.

Buildings always had a maintenance manager, who often had a maintenance staff. The maintenance man usually reported to a property manager who oversaw everything. Then, depending on size, the property manager reported to a regional manager, who would then report to corporate.

We made a concerted effort to get everyone in that chain of command on our side. We established multiple touchpoints within every customer organization. Why?

Let's say we cut a deal with a customer at the corporate level. That one touchpoint was clearly very important to make the deal—but who else in that organization needed to buy into this new agreement for it to be successful?

How about the regional manager or the property manager or (most importantly) the maintenance manager? You need all of them on your side if you want your relationship to run smoothly.

That's what I mean by selling through the organization. We could have made our best sales pitch at the corporate level, but if the maintenance person didn't like us—guess what? We'd have an uphill battle to sell him or her on it! Make it easy on yourself by selling to every level in a given organization.

This lesson can be tied back to the advice to pay attention to the second in charge. There is so much turnover in modern business today, you can't assume your one connection, no matter how strategically placed, is going to stay there forever. Prepare for the inevitable changing of the guard by selling your services at every level.

70: PEACE-OF-MIND SALES

The goal of all of these sales strategies is to give your customers peace of mind. If you can do that consistently, you will create raving fans of your work, who will continue to do business with your company just to keep having that sense of security.

When maintenance managers and staff were doing business with Wilmar, they knew we were there for them if their inventory ran short. They knew our salespeople would do anything to help.

This kind of comfort level sets the stage for "peace of mind" sales.

These sales happen after you have proved to a client beyond any doubt that you've got their back. From then on, your peace-of-mind clients will get all warm and fuzzy when they think of your business and keep coming back.

Any type of business can offer peace of mind to its customers. Case in point: we're giving peace of mind to our LendingOne customers. Our clients, who are all real estate investors, know they can start shopping for properties and in ten to fourteen days will have the money to close on whatever property they choose. This gives our customers that secure and comfortable feeling that is pure gold.

71: MASTER "RELATIONSHIP SELLING"

"Relationship selling" was one of the things we did pretty well at Wilmar. Looking back, I'd say it was how I laid the foundation for our entire business. I wanted to create raving fans of our work. Well, raving fans do not come from casual acquaintanceships; they come from forming an emotional bond with customers that grows until they become fanatics who can't get enough of what you're serving.

I've spent most of my career trying to master "relationship selling"; I can't say I have yet, but I'm still working on it! It would bode well for your career if you tried to master it, too.

During my Wilmar years, I was responsible for the corporate relationships with our largest customers. I was the resident rainmaker, who absolutely loved landing the big fish. I felt an amazing high every time I got one in the boat. I was hooked on making deals!

What was my secret to success? That's easy. I was able to develop strong and sticky relationships with pretty much every big customer I had. Of course, we also had to offer fair prices and great service to land their business, but I wasn't naïve to the fact that our big clients could always take their business elsewhere. I knew we had some very formidable competitors, so I treated all big customers like they were VIPs.

I still treat my best customers like VIPs, even today at LendingOne. It makes absolutely no difference what line of business you are in. Making someone feel good never gets old. That's why "relationship selling" will always rule—so get schmoozing!

Anytime you have big clients on the hook, roll out the red carpet and make them feel super confident in your relationship. Bend over backward for them. Once you have convinced them that you sincerely care about their business, they will love you forever and keep coming back.

72: EMBRACE THE POWER OF NETWORKING

If you want to become a master at relationship selling, you should first embrace the power of networking. It is so important if you want your business to soar. Networking isn't everything, but it's pretty close. Without networking, you have no relationships. And without relationships, you have no raving fans of your work. And without raving fans of your work? You're dead!

So learn to network.

Can you believe I learned a great lesson about networking while watching a basketball game? As a fan of the Philadelphia 76ers, I've attended a lot of their games over my lifetime. I was elated when I first got my season tickets in 1987. My seats weren't courtside yet, but they were close enough to the action that I could see everything going on around the benches.

I kept spotting the same impressive-looking young man at game after game. He knew how to work the crowd like a pro. He was always talking to all the players and coaches. Maybe it was his confident strut, but I found myself watching him during the time-outs. He was too young to be an ex-player or a coach, and he didn't seem to be an agent, yet he knew every player in the NBA. I thought, *Who is this guy?*

One evening at a Sixers game, I saw my good friend Leon Rose chatting with this mystery man. That was it. I needed to find out who this guy was, so I walked over to Leon, a Cherry Hill attorney who helped negotiate a large warehouse lease for Wilmar, and I asked him about "the guy."

"That's Wes," Leon said.

I asked, "Wes who?"

Leon said, "He just goes by 'Wes.' He's friends with all of the players. Let me introduce you."

So, Leon introduces my wife Amy and me to Wes over dinner at Ovations, the upscale restaurant in the Spectrum (where the Sixers used to play). I found out the mystery man had a full name: William Wesley from Merchantville, New Jersey. Wes and I bonded immediately and became great friends.

As time went on, I noticed Wes was a networking genius. He said he was a mortgage broker, but after watching him work his magic, I could tell he was connected to professional sports in some way. The more I hung out with the guy, the clearer it became that Wes was one of the most powerful men in sports. I'm not exaggerating. In March 2005, Scoop Jackson wrote in ESPN's "Page 2" column: "I believe Phil Knight (the CEO of Nike) is the most powerful man in sports, next to William Wesley." Some mortgage broker! He was and is a power broker, and he's even been mentioned in rap songs by Drake and Jay-Z. Does it get any bigger than that?

I consider myself a pretty well-connected guy in the world of business, but Wes's circle of connections in the sports and business world is even bigger than mine!

Through Wes's massive networking circle, I've been able to meet enough NBA players to fill up a Hall of Fame. When Michael Jordan was still playing for the Bulls, Wes lived in Chicago, so anytime I was in Chicago on business, Wes and I would connect. He introduced me to a lot of players. I was like a kid in a candy store getting to meet NBA legends like Michael Jordan, Scottie Pippen, Allen Iverson, Mark Aguirre, Allan Houston, Charles Oakley, Shaquille O'Neal, LeBron James, Eddie Jones, Derek Coleman, and Ron Harper, to name a few.

I remember the first time I met Michael Jordan, the greatest player that ever lived, if you ask me. It was the only time I was so in awe of a person that I was speechless.

All these years later, Wes is still an amazing example of the power of networking. Google his nickname, "World Wide Wes," if you want to read more about the influence he unofficially wields in the sports world. Wes has built an empire from the ground up through the sheer strength of relationships.

How did he do it?

Wes doesn't divulge his secrets, but I imagine his clients

trust him with their lives (and livelihoods) because he gets the job done, period. That's why his name gets dropped in Drake and Jay-Z songs. Wes has networked himself everywhere. I remember back in the 1999/2000 basketball season, Wes introduced me to the assistant coach for the Sixers (now famous), John Calipari. Fast-forward to a few years later and John Calipari, Wes, and I are talking hoops over lunch at Ozzie's at Longport. That, my friends, is how networking works!

Where is Wes today?

First, I have to tell you about what happened to Leon Rose, my good friend who connected us. The first time I met with Leon back in 1990, he was in his office and had a basketball on his desk, which was a great conversation starter. He told me that he wanted to become an NBA player's agent one day. Back in 1990, that dream job sounded a little far-fetched for anyone to achieve, even a successful lawyer like Leon. I told him, "Cool. Good luck with that."

Guess what?

Leon has gone on to become one of the biggest agents in the NBA! Today, Leon runs the basketball division for Creative Artists Agency (CAA) and represents players like Carmelo Anthony, Chris Paul, (formerly) LeBron James, and retired players like Allen Iverson, Richard Hamilton, and Eddie Jones.

Leon made his dream come true. I am so proud of you, man.

As for World Wide Wes? The legend is better than ever, unofficially still working his under-the-radar magic. What's he doing officially? Man, you know Wes. The only title Wes officially has today is "Consultant at CAA."

Here is an epilogue, just to give you a sense of Wes's memory and people skills. A few weeks ago as I write this, Amy and I were having dinner with Wes, Leon, and Leon's wife, Donna, at the Jersey Shore. We started reminiscing about the times we hung out before and after games at Ovations. The Sixers moved to a new stadium in 1996, so the Spectrum and Ovations have been closed for more than twenty years.

Well, Amy asked the table, "What was the maître d's name who was always so nice?" Leon, Donna, and I looked at each other; we didn't have a clue. Guess who did?

"That was Cliff," Wes said casually.

See? Wes never forgets anybody. And that's part of what makes him great. He is truly one of the best networkers I have ever met in my life. Wes is an outstanding example to pattern your career after if you want to become a true networking master.

And who doesn't want to be the ruler of his or her domain?

73: POUNCE ON YOUR COMPETITION'S WEAKNESSES

I know I have said not to pay attention to what the outside world thinks, but that doesn't mean to ignore your competitors. That's the kiss of death.

Have you ever read *The Art of War* by Sun Tzu? If you haven't, you should.

"If you know the enemy and know yourself, you need not fear the result of a hundred battles." That Sun Tzu guy was onto something.

Never forget your competitors are your enemy. This really ties back to Lesson #40: "Take advantage of competitor misses." You absolutely have to know them better than even your allies. The goal is to know your competition's strengths and weaknesses like they were your own. Once you know your competitors' soft spots, your sales team will have the ammo to pounce on them.

We all run into customers who tell us what our competitors are doing, so listen up and take notes. The only way to respond to customers who speak fondly about your competition is to hit them with facts that deflate their argument and support yours. The only way to have these facts at your fingertips is to dissect your competitors like they were frogs in biology class.

Find out what makes your competitors tick.

Know what your customers are seeing in the marketplace.

Once you see what your competitors do well—and what they do not—then you can begin to exploit their weaknesses by bolstering your offering in areas your competitors are weakest.

For example, what if a competitor is clearly having trouble making next-day deliveries? What do you do next? Do I have to spell it out for you? You put pressure on them by offering same-day delivery yourself. I know that sounds cutthroat, but that's business.

74: HE WHO DOES HIS HOMEWORK
MAKES THE MOST SALES

I realize I'm always preaching "Do your homework." Some of you may be wondering if this is my way of making up for the fact I never went to college. Not quite. Doing homework has been a quantifiable best practice throughout my entire life. I may not have been the best student in high school, but I sure as heck knew how to do my homework in real life. You should too.

At Wilmar, we did our homework and then some, and it paid innumerable dividends over the years. I cannot list the million different ways that doing our homework helped us make a sale, but here is one good example.

After talking to a lot of our large customers, we learned what an apartment owner spent on average per unit on maintenance supplies each year. This was crucial intelligence for us, because we were always trying to get our customer's "entire wallet share."

So now we knew what most apartment complexes should be spending, by size and age. If they ended up spending less than their annual budget with us, we knew they were probably buying the other products from one of our competitors.

Knowing all of this information was huge.

You better believe we instructed our sales team to circle back to customers who were still doing business with our competitors. Sometimes it worked, and sometimes it didn't. But it is still a good best practice to instill in any company.

In fact, doing "deep background" on our customers worked out so well for us at Wilmar, I instituted the same best practices at LendingOne. Yes, it works a little differently, but the results are the same.

What do I mean?

When someone buys a property or takes out a mortgage, those transactions are all public record, right? So by "doing our homework" and looking at public records, we can find out how many properties a particular individual bought and sold in the last year. Let's say I find out a customer is doing twenty deals per year—but LendingOne is only involved in five of them. That makes me curious. I wonder, "Hmm, who is getting this customer's business for the other fifteen deals?"

So I tell my team to make a note of it. And if this client finances a property through us and we don't hear from him or her again for a few months, I challenge my team to go out and get the rest of this client's business.

See how valuable information can be? All of this proactive action would not have been possible unless I had done my homework.

Knowing is half the battle.

75: NAIL YOUR SALES BY DOING IT DIFFERENTLY

When it comes to sales, firms that successfully differentiate themselves are rewarded for their uniqueness—whether it's in their products, in their delivery system, or in their quality of service. The company that does it differently usually stands out.

I'll say it again: if you want to help your sales team make sales, find a way to stand out in the crowded marketplace. Believe me, it will give them the ammunition they need to close the deal.

Think about it. If you do everything that your competitors do and nothing else, what are your sales reps' talking points going to be when they're pitching potential new customers? You have to find that special something that you and you alone can do, then do it better than anyone else.

How did we differentiate ourselves at Wilmar?

One way we did it was through something we called "shop management programs." No one was offering anything like them at the time. Remember how our biggest customers were maintenance men? Did we do our homework on them! We found out everything about them, and then we took that information and used it to create a program for them. Our research told us that no one makes maintenance workers feel special, so we set out to be the first company that did.

We learned maintenance staff were not very good at inventory control, so we thought about how we could make their lives easier. We developed a shop management program just for that purpose. It was sort of like a maintenance boot camp to get their shops in order.

The first thing we did when people signed up for the program was to send a sales rep out to visit them and help organize their shop. The maintenance guys loved this program!

Another way we differentiated ourselves in the marketplace was to create a massive special-order business. So when customers came to us who needed something that was not in our catalogue, we had an entire department dedicated to finding that rare and unique product for them.

Again, no one else was doing this at the time.

All of these programs were so unique that CNBC featured them in a 1998 special about Wilmar. I was pretty proud of that CNBC show. Do you think that if we didn't have those special programs, we would have been featured? I can't answer that for certain, but I can say Wilmar made a much more interesting story by standing out from the crowd.

76: GUERRILLA NEGOTIATING

I want to add one final wrinkle to our sales conversation that few people seem to get these days. Sales is not just about selling to the individual; you have to negotiate with vendors or suppliers, too. I have no idea whether you work with suppliers in your line of business, but if you do, how you negotiate with them directly affects your profitability.

Anybody can cut prices, right? But for it to work, you have to make a profit doing it. You have to be extremely smart about how you purchase your products. Never let a vendor get too comfortable with your relationship. Never stop exploring alternatives.

I feel like this is something we did incredibly well at Wilmar, so much so that I've continued to push it in every business I touch. I call my vendor negotiating skills *guerrilla negotiation*.

When you are guerrilla negotiating, you should approach all your vendor negotiations from a win-win perspective. You don't want to beat the crap out of a vendor. Why? If you are killing vendors on every deal, they will go out of business or take their business elsewhere where they can make a profit!

This is not good for you or your vendor.

Ideally, you want to cultivate a lineup of profitable, happy vendors. When your vendors are happy, they will continue to serve you, which is more important than squeezing out every last penny on every deal.

THREE CATEGORIES OF VENDOR NEGOTIATION

When it comes to negotiating with vendors, here is how I would approach them. I've found negotiations come in three categories—and each one requires a different tactic:

1. Commodity Product (or Service) Negotiations— This will be your easiest type of negotiation because the vendor knows you have a lot of options. Why? Commodity products can be made by any number of suppliers. Your customers do not care where they come from. There are no brand names attached: think screws, nuts, or bolts. At Wilmar, when we needed some type of generic widget, negotiations were not difficult, because I could choose from many suppliers, domestic and abroad. What if you can't settle on a price? You have all the leverage. You can move on to another supplier or, if you have the means, even create your own generic widget brand.
2. Brand Name with Options Negotiations—Now, let's say you only need to offer one specific product, but your customers want to know that product comes from a strong brand. You may think you don't have any leverage, but you do! I remember back at Wilmar, we could have stocked lightbulbs from every quality brand out there, but we only needed one. Why not offer them all? There was no need! I knew our customers would buy any of them, so I negotiated with all of the best brands (Sylvania, GE, and Philips) and leveraged them against each other until I got the best price. What if I didn't find a vendor I liked? Wilmar would pull out of negotiations and simply create our

own private label brand for a lower cost but with higher profit margins. Talk about options.

3. Brand-Name Negotiations—We all know big brand names are extremely important to a lot of customers (think Coke, Disney, and Apple). That's why they're huge companies, because people swear by them. So how do you negotiate in the big leagues? The first rule is, you no longer have leverage! You can't play hardball. Instead of attempting a "full silverback" maneuver on a giant corporation that could eat you for breakfast, you should try to negotiate a win-win partnership for you both. You may not get the lowest possible price per unit (you never do when buying name brands), but you can offset the higher buy cost by adding value to your relationship. You may be able to negotiate a better price if you help your brand-name vendor enter a new market; they love doing that! You could also get a better price by improving your buying patterns, doing things like buying in bulk to help your brand-name vendor offset costs of doing business with you. That way, you save your vendor money, and those savings can be passed on to you.

The bottom line is, if you can put as much time and effort into mastering vendor negotiations as you do selling to your individual customers, I can promise you it's going to be a win-win situation for everyone involved. Your vendors will thank you. Your customers will thank you.

And your bottom line will thank you too.

THE BENEFITS OF OVERSEAS IMPORTING

I know some people believe you should always "buy American" and I agree with that notion (to a degree) but sometimes it's just not realistic—so don't rule out importing your products from overseas without investigating the possibility. Many of the largest US companies already have their proprietary products manufactured overseas. There is also a huge flow of products (whose patents have run out) that are being copied like mad internationally. The importing business is booming overseas.

I can't say the quality is better with foreign products or services; but if (for example) an Asian manufacturer can produce your item for a lower cost and the product is almost identical to that of higher-priced manufacturers in the United States (and the Asian manufacturer is not running a sweatshop), I'd say to "go for it" as long as you can be sure of two things:

1. You Aren't Skimping on Quality—You have to do a great job of "quality control" when it comes to monitoring the work of your overseas partners. If the quality of your goods goes down and your customers notice the difference—what was the point of saving a few bucks when the end result is you are now losing more customers because your products suddenly stink?
2. You Make It Worth Your While—Don't pull the trigger on an overseas manufacturer unless you're sure your gross margins can be significantly increased. If your numbers don't add up, then it's a no-brainer—stick with your US manufacturers.

CUTTING OUT THE MIDDLEMAN

In Wilmar's early days, we bought quite a few products from companies that positioned themselves as manufacturers but were really importers. They were "middlemen" who didn't build anything themselves. `

When I saw what they were up to, I thought, *We can do that too*. So Wilmar decided to become an "importer." We began manufacturing several of our "private label" products in Asia. By importing the products ourselves, we were able to make the margins that our "middlemen" used to. Being a direct importer from the very early stages of the company gave us a big competitive advantage, but like everything in business, "The devil is in the details."

You have to be running a tight ship.

It can take up to ninety days for an Asian product to arrive on our shores so you have to be highly organized to keep track of it all. You need a "proven" automated backend process in place, or it can be a challenge from an inventory perspective. Remember to put a pencil to all these savings! For every penny you save on the overseas manufacturing costs, you will have to pay more for things like port charges, freight services, duty fees, taxes, and bank charges.

KEY TAKEAWAYS

- Great salespeople are high-energy, confident, hungry to earn, knowledgeable, and inclined to see obstacles as challenges.
- Hire salespeople who are confident and comfortable with client maintenance. Clients smell sincerity, and your representatives must be sincere in everything they do.
- Client engagement is critical to overall success, and there are many ways of achieving that.
- Be persistent with clients and you'll make lifelong customers.
- Peace of mind and relationship selling are foundational to any successful business.
- Without networking, you have no relationships. Network!
- Your competition is your enemy; learn their weaknesses and pounce.
- Guerilla negotiating means being willing to negotiate from a new perspective.

CHAPTER 8

TAKING YOUR BUSINESS TO THE NEXT LEVEL

How dare you settle for less when the world made it so easy for you to be remarkable?

—Seth Godin, best-selling author

GOOD IS NOT GOOD ENOUGH: DARE TO BE GREAT

Now that you have your company firing on all cylinders, the onus is on you to step up and become a great CEO. No pressure, but that's what this chapter is all about—taking your company and yourself to the next level.

Why do I care so much about being great? Do I have some kind of inferiority complex? C'mon. My passion for greatness boils down to this: we don't need any more mediocre products and services in the world. What we need are more great people producing great things. My goal with this book is to inspire you to be the next great entrepreneur.

Are you still with me? Awesome! Let's roll up our sleeves and get to work.

77: BECOME A TACTICAL
AND STRATEGIC CEO

Let me ask you this: how can you create a sustainable growth business that keeps cranking out an amazing product or service every year, that people will keep running over their grandmothers on Black Friday to get?

Keep raising your game every day.

Keep reaching for the next rung on the ladder.

Never stop climbing.

I know what some of you are saying. "But Bill, you've got me maxing out. My arms aren't long enough to reach that next rung!"

I'll give you a minute to catch your breath, but you can't have a self-defeating attitude or you may as well close up shop and go work for somebody else!

You've got to think bigger than what the average person thinks is possible. The first thing you should do is adopt a trait that all the great CEOs exhibit and become skilled at making both strategic and tactical decisions. What's the difference?

Tactical leadership is doing things right.

Strategic leadership is doing the right things.

I know you must be doing a lot of things right tactically to get your startup off the ground. Great job, but now it's time to think about your long-term strategy. You can't get behind the curve on anything.

The greatest CEOs are visionaries, not just one-trick ponies; they're always plotting their company's next big move. Bold innovators are rewarded in this "drone-eat-dog" world, so if you see a way to improve your business, you'd better have the vision and the guts to pull the trigger, even if the naysayers say it can't be done.

You will also be better able to execute. Any coach will tell you that. Don't forget that, while you're gazing into your crystal ball, you also have to keep operating your business, and that's where your tactical leadership comes into play. Your goal should be to kick so much butt that your competition isn't even thinking about the future. Why? They're too busy trying to keep up with all the stuff you're doing right now.

See how one skill plays into the other? Strategy-tactics is the yin-yang of corporate leadership. Having the ability to do both extremely well is mental multitasking of the highest degree. It's all about having one foot in the now and one foot in the future.

EXPERIENCE PLUS WISDOM EQUALS STRATEGY

If you're like me, it may take some time to learn to be a great strategic leader. Like a lot of fresh-faced entrepreneurs, I was a very good tactical manager when I was young. In my early years at Wilmar, I got things done. You want a catalogue out? Boom, boom, boom! I was going to build you a catalogue.

But I was so inexperienced, I didn't necessarily have a robust vision for the future. Looking back, I didn't know a lot of things, but I made up for my shortcomings with energy, effort, and enthusiasm. My motto was, "Grrr, get out of the way!" And it worked in those early years—but I couldn't sustain it and expect to remain successful.

So I worked on becoming a more strategic leader. How?

Let's go back to the catalogue example. I created this amazing catalogue (which became our signature calling card) literally by hand, because that's the way you did it back then. I wanted it to be perfect, but didn't think about the fact that I had to recreate that sucker every year. I had built a blueprint that was successful, but wasn't sustainable.

So I formed a strategy for making the catalogues.

First, I bought a Mac and started creating them on PageMaker. Then, the moment the company could afford it, I delegated them tactically, but never strategically. I had other employees create the catalogues, but everything that went in them still crossed my desk. I had precise rules for formatting and content, as well as an open-door policy, so I managed the process all along the way.

I didn't wait for the entire 700-page catalogue to be completed; I oversaw it incrementally a few pages at a time so I could correct problems and make small changes. See what I'm talking about? If you learn how to manage properly, you can be a delegating hands-off strategic leader while also keeping your hands on the tactical stuff.

That's just one example of how you have to use both sides of your brain when leading a company in the future. It's vital that you learn to apply a strategic-tactical mindset to every part of your company, be it your team, your operations, your R&D, your marketing, your sales, your technology, or your customer service.

The bottom line is that every successful CEO is a good tactician, but if you aren't being smart about how you lead your business into tomorrow, you may look up one day and realize you're building bicycles in a world full of hoverboards!

78: A HEALTHY COMPANY CAN GROW ORGANICALLY

One of the things the strategic side of your brain should always be thinking about is how you are going to grow your business—because if you aren't growing, you're stagnating, you're fossilizing, you're dying a slow death.

I personally believe a healthy company can grow organically. I know a lot of CEOs will tell you that you can acquire other businesses and grow just fine that way, but I don't think that is always true. Following that strategy is like trying to build your entire NBA team through free agency instead of drafting wisely. What happens when the checkbook is gone? You're screwed, right?

But it remains a popular route to take. I still run into a lot of business owners who tell me, "We're not growing, so we need to go buy a company." Seriously? If you're going to manage this new company the same way you've been running your business that isn't growing, you're going to get the same mediocre results, only on a larger scale.

I'm not saying acquisitions aren't a nice way to grow (they are), but you can't buy yourself out of trouble. You shouldn't buy a competitor until you get your own house together. A house on a weak foundation will cave in!

I truly believe the organic growth of a company is a great indicator of its overall health; I really walked the walk on organic growth in my early years. Before we did our first acquisition at the end of 1995, Wilmar/Interline grew organically at an average of 30 percent per year. And even after we began buying our smaller competitors, we still maintained a strong double-digit organic growth model.

Now that's healthy living.

79: HAVE A DUAL BUSINESS STRATEGY

But sometimes there are great opportunities out there that you just can't turn down. That's why I'm a big believer in having a dual strategy for how to grow your company. I say, grow organically as long as you can—but you can only go so long eating from your homegrown garden before you have to sharpen your claws and devour a competitor. If you find an opportunity to acquire a business that is going to fill a void in your service offering or your geographical reach, don't be gun-shy just because it's not a totally organic deal.

Sometimes, it's good to buy nonorganic.

This is especially true in today's marketplace where, let's face it, every player in the game is forming alliances and either looking to acquire companies or be acquired. It's the law of the jungle. Eat or be eaten. You can't change the rules. You can only live by them.

I know every company is different, but I'm telling you, we followed this dual strategy during Wilmar's acquisition years, and it really paid off. We grew organically for the most part, but I didn't flinch when it was time to become a part-time carnivore. I took the plunge and found that I loved the taste of fresh meat.

Here is how I applied a dual strategy to every growth opportunity that came our way. It was pretty simple. After we targeted a new untapped geographic market, the first thing we did was try to inflict some pain on our regional competitors through a direct-mail marketing assault. We would hire a few salespeople to infiltrate the area so the local competitors knew we were coming. Once they were afraid of us, if we saw a viable acquisition target in the market we'd try to buy that competitor.

What if we couldn't make a deal?

We switched strategies, opened a new warehouse in that city, and took on our local competition that way. In some cases, we were successful at buying our competition. In other cases, we weren't and had to open up a warehouse.

The point is: either way, we had a plan.

I don't know what growth looks like in your business, but I'm telling you, don't put all your eggs in one basket when it comes to taking that next big leap. Adopt a dual strategy (part organic growth, part "red meat" acquisitions), and create a healthy diet if you want to stay in the ring with any heavyweight that gets in your path.

If not, prepare to be some other carnivore's main course.

CLIMBING THE SUMMIT WITH SUMMIT PARTNERS

I'll talk more about our acquisitions later, but let's not get ahead of ourselves. There we were, in 1995. Wilmar was doing a great job competing against the biggest players in the industry. We were being smart while growing organically and investigating whether we should acquire smaller companies. We still hadn't pulled the trigger on any deals—and then something interesting happened.

I got approached by Summit Partners, a prestigious private equity firm with billions of dollars under management. They told me they wanted to buy 55 percent of the company. This was a new proposition altogether.

They weren't one of our competitors who wanted to swallow us up; they wanted to invest in Wilmar and buy a majority ownership stake. Summit offered me twenty-two million bucks. Their pitch was, "as, sell us 55 percent and take some of your chips off the table. After your family is taken care of and you're set for life, let's go out and really grow this thing, and you won't have to worry about risk."

I went home and thought, *Oh my God—that's more money than I could ever have imagined earning in my life—and yet, I'd still own 45 percent of the company.*

What was I going to do?

It was a huge decision. I'd always been the big kahuna, so bringing Summit into the mix could be a huge change for me. I wondered, *Were they even offering me the right price?* I know it sounds crazy, but I didn't hire an investment banker to help me with the valuation of my company. Back in 1995, I didn't even know what an investment banker was!

After talking to my attorney, researching private company valuations and doing some more negotiating with Summit, I determined they were offering me a pretty fair price—so I went home and thought long and hard about it. I talked it over with my wife Amy and decided, *You know what? This is a good move.*

Could I have gotten a little more money if I'd hired an investment banker? Probably. If I were making that deal today, would I do it any differently? Absolutely. I learned a long time ago that the only way you can get an accurate valuation for your company is to let the market tell you what it's worth. You can't just take the first offer that comes along.

But this time, I did.

And even though I wasn't super savvy about how I handled my first rodeo—guess what? The Summit deal turned out great. You may ask, "Are you just saying that because you got to take care of your family?"

Sure, it was great to finally get paid. I'd been paying myself peanuts compared to other CEOs of companies my size for eighteen years and putting it all back into the growth of the company. But that wasn't the only reason the deal with Summit was so good.

It was also a great strategic move.

I knew the Summit partnership was going to make us championship material, and I didn't want to settle for anything other than the big brass ring. It was a win-win decision for the company and me personally—and those are the best deals you can make.

The only concern I had was the control factor. I was still a total control freak at the time. While the Summit acquisition was going to take us to the next level and make us bigger, was I going to miss having total control over the company? This was a big deal, because I never had any other advisors in the business besides my dad, Fred, and for a short time, Abby.

Could I let go?

GOING PUBLIC MY WAY

Turned out, there was nothing to worry about. Summit let me do my thing. The only thing they ever advised me on was how (and when) to go public, which had been a dream of mine since I was a young kid. I mean, if you were on the NYSE or NASDAQ, it meant you had arrived and were somebody, right? But that was just a childhood dream. Was going public the right move, strategically?

At first, I thought the timing wasn't great.

The Summit deal was only ten months old, and I was already working on our first acquisition. The company was called OneSource Supply, and it was based in Hollywood, Florida.

After meeting with them, I told Summit, "I want to offer these guys four million bucks for their company."

The board approved the acquisition, but after the meeting, the Summit board representative Ernest Jacquet called me up and said, "We need to go public now."

I said, "Let me get my first acquisition tucked in first. Then we'll go public."

"Bill, if you screw up this acquisition and the integration, you'll never go public."

I thought about it and said, "What if we do them both at the same time?"

"If you make that first acquisition part of the IPO story, you're going to get a great valuation."

Ernest was right. We set the wheels in motion on the IPO and acquisition simultaneously.

The next thing I knew, we were working with a team of investment bankers (from Alex. Brown & Sons, Paine Webber, William Blair & Company, and Robertson Stevens) who were all vying to be the lead banker and underwrite the deal. We ended up going with Alex. Brown & Sons as our lead banker, but all of the investment bankers in the running remained part of the IPO.

What did I know about having that many investment banks involved? The answer was, nothing really!

But it worked out great because I trusted my advisors. All the investment bankers on the IPO team helped me craft an amazing IPO story, and since we had profit margins like a retailer (but didn't have any stores) Wilmar fell into the category of "business-to-business non-store retailers," which made our IPO story even more unique.

We were going public my way.

Wilmar bought One Source Supply on Thursday, November 16, 1995.

Wilmar filed with the SEC to go public the following Monday.

Just like that. On January 6, 1996, we started the IPO road show in New York and traveled to all of the large financial cities in the United States, United Kingdom, and Switzerland. Wilmar was priced at eleven dollars to institutional investors, friends, and family and opened trading at fifteen dollars, which was a huge first-day stock pop back then.

It was an awesome experience.

RUNNING A PUBLIC COMPANY VERSUS RUNNING A PRIVATE COMPANY

What is better: running a private or publicly held company? People ask me this question all the time, and I say, pick your poison! Do you want to catch hell in the newspapers or just in the boardroom? There's no escape when you are running a big company. Unless you are a 100 percent owner, that's the game you have to play, either way you go.

I will say, being a publicly traded company was really interesting. I didn't necessarily love it, but I've got to tell you, the people I met and the knowledge I gained were amazing. It was rare for someone my age (thirty-seven) to run a public company back then. I know that, with the current tech boom, there are a zillion people in their twenties going public now, but back then, it was pretty unusual.

THE UPSIDE OF HAVING A VALUE-ADDED BOARD

One advantage of going public is you have an opportunity to have a talented board of directors that adds value to your business. My partners over at Summit helped me recruit a few new members for Wilmar's board shortly after we went public. I'm telling you, having an amazing board is such a great luxury; I'm pretty sure it would never have happened if we had stayed private.

One big-time businessman who added value to our company was Martin "Marty" Hanaka, who is still a great friend. He was the president of Staples, the office supply company, when he came onboard. Why was Marty such a good board member?

First of all, our businesses had a lot in common. You wouldn't think that at first glance, since Staples had retail stores, but we both served commercial clients, both of our businesses had great catalogues, and we both had field sales forces.

Even our inventory was similar.

Both of our companies were selling products that ranged from tiny in size (like paper clips or screws) to large (like desks or water heaters). Having an inventory with diverse physical characteristics created challenges in warehousing and distribution, which meant we could relate to each other!

Needless to say, I relied on Marty as a sounding board and mentor during my time as CEO of a publicly traded company. Marty has gone on to become CEO of Sports Authority and then Golfsmith, so he's had a pretty great career since he served on my board. But I'm sure glad he did. His input made Wilmar better—and none of that would have been possible if we had not gone public.

80: YOUR SHAREHOLDERS WILL OWN YOU IF YOU LET THEM

Of course, I also had a love/hate relationship with being public. As much as it was really cool, some of it also sucked!

If you go public, you'll never know who to trust.

Even though investors will tell you that they are long-term investors who are in it for the duration, don't believe them. They're full of it. If you miss a quarter, they'll be selling your stock. There is no loyalty when money is involved.

That was my first wake-up call. I had surrounded myself with loyal employees and had built a raving-fan base of loyal customers in the eighteen years we were a private company, so having to deal with the nonbelievers was not exactly fun. But it's part of the game you bought into . . . Know that.

Get in that CEO chair and you will find that your shareholders not only own a portion of your company, but they also think they own a portion of you. I felt like I had to be at their service 24/7. The big conundrum I grappled with every day was, *Do I spend my time worrying about serving Main Street or Wall Street?* I've always loved my customers and tried to make myself very accessible to them—but I also knew where to draw the line.

Going public was a completely different animal.

I don't want to sound like a petulant brat here, but when I'm not traveling, I make it a priority to have dinner at home with Amy and the kids every night. Well, that goes out the window when you're running a public company! Tell your kids you'll see them on weekends, hopefully. I know this may not sound like a gigantic deal (we all miss dinners no matter what jobs we have), but I really love my family and not seeing them except mostly on weekends was a big downside to going public, at least to me.

I didn't live at the office like some lawyers do who work a hundred hours a week, but I did spend an inordinate amount of time talking to shareholders. I realize some companies have a CFO who could have fielded some of these calls, but I didn't at Wilmar. Sure, I had a CFO who was a smart guy, but talking to shareholders wasn't his thing. And since CFOs usually talk to Wall Street, guess who had to deal with all the banks and the shareholders? Me!

I spearheaded all the investor relations, so I wound up on the phone quite a bit with the likes of people from Fidelity or Janus Funds, who each owned 10 percent of the company. I know what you're saying. "Poor me," right?

Okay, maybe part of it was me.

Maybe I was too emotionally invested in the company

because it was my pride and joy. Maybe some CEOs would have had no problem drawing boundaries for their personal lives, but not me. I didn't want to lose a single shareholder.

And when I did, I really took it to heart. I cared, man.

Maybe a little too much.

ANALYSTS ALSO OWN YOU

I don't want to make you paranoid about going public, but your shareholders aren't the only ones breathing down your CEO collar. At Wilmar, every investment bank that was part of our IPO had an analyst who covered our company. And you can't ignore the analysts. They are another group of people you need to serve. They want and need details on your business so they can do their jobs. Trust me, it is in your best interest to comply.

As CEO of a public company, you have to keep tabs on your "analysts' estimates" and "put out fires" whenever an analyst gives your company a less-than-optimistic outlook. I also spent a lot of time speaking at investment banking conferences. Yes, it was time-consuming, but it did make me very comfortable speaking about my business in front of large groups.

If you don't learn to speak proficiently about your business, you will not be publicly traded for long.

EVERYONE KNOWS YOUR BUSINESS

You may have gathered that running a public company means you work too hard. Luckily, I was young, so I didn't drop dead of a heart attack from all the stress, but no matter how old you are, you will find it's a real challenge to strike a healthy life balance, especially if you are a workaholic. It was for me, and I'm a workaholic family man who had done pretty well at balancing both worlds up to that point.

But when we went public, I had less time for my wife and kids, and zero time for my time-consuming hobbies. From 1990 to 1994, I had run five marathons and dozens of triathlons, but now I had to stop doing them. I just didn't have time to compete at the level I was accustomed to, and that hurt because I'm a pretty competitive guy.

So what did I do?

I joined the local country club to play golf, which in my wildest dreams I had never thought I could afford. I wasn't one of those guys who liked to hang around the nineteenth-hole bar, but there I'd be on a Saturday morning, trying to relax with a bunch of guys around the tee box. Somebody would come up to me and say, "Hey I see you made an acquisition," or "I read your sales for the quarter were off."

I'd just smile and think, *Are you kidding me?* Of the twenty quarters Wilmar was a publicly traded company, we missed our numbers just one time, and this was what I got? It's not like I was embarrassed to talk about the business; I just wanted to tell these guys, "You know what, it's Saturday morning. I don't feel like talking about this stuff."

But I kept it inside. I answered every question. I knew what the tradeoff was; I was the public face of the company now. I told myself, "Just deal with it," and I did.

But it slowly wore me down.

I'm a pretty private guy, and I could never escape the spotlight. Everybody knew everything that was going on in my business. And when I say "everything," I mean "everything." They call it "going public" for a reason.

When we announced in 2000 that we were going back to being a private company, there was a big article on the front page of the Business Section of the *Philadelphia Inquirer* about Wilmar, with graphs and pie charts that basically divulged my entire financial status to the world. I felt like my privacy was violated, but what could I do about it? That is part of the package when you go public. Everything your business does is laid bare for the world to see, including your own finances.

HUNTING TROLLS ON SOCIAL MEDIA

In addition to the traditional media, you can't forget about dealing with the trolls on social media. Every business has them. We didn't have Facebook or Twitter back when Wilmar was public—but there were the Yahoo Message Boards, which used to drive me nuts.

Like any social media platform, anyone could write anything about your business, whether it was true or not. I remember one false claim that got me so irritated I hired a private detective to discount it. Wilmar had gotten so good at "relationship selling," some anonymous commenter on the Yahoo board accused us of "greasing the wheels" to win the business of our largest customers, which was completely untrue. So I hired a cyber-sleuth and found out the yahoo who was trolling us on the message board was a sales manager at one of our competitors!

All of this is part of the "going public" package. Sounds like a blast, right?

It's not always fun, but that's why they pay you the big bucks. If you can't develop a thick skin for this kind of stuff, then you better get off the stage and out of the public arena, because it never stops coming.

HOW TO SEEK STRATEGIC ALTERNATIVES

I was cool with being in the spotlight for five years, and then I said, "You know what? I think I may be ready to do something different." Personally, I felt my time as the CEO of an independent, publicly traded company was counting down. The more successful we got, it was only a matter of time before we were forcibly acquired.

There are companies out there that are "too big to fail," but there is no company on earth that is too big to merge. But what was the right move for Wilmar? Eat or be eaten?

When you're doing business in a market full of predators, it comes down to whether you have the financial power to eat up other companies or the strategic moxie to align yourself with a bigger one. Even when you are riding high as the CEO, you should always be reevaluating your strategy to see if there's a better road to success. Strategic alliances are an integral part of the game—and by 1998, I had my eyes wide open: I wanted to change.

Wilmar was in our third year of being public: we had reached $193 million in sales. Our stock was doing pretty well, but not as well as I wanted. I wanted to be great.

One of the problems was that I didn't I feel like we were getting respect from Wall Street because we weren't a sexy investment like some of the tech stocks out there. I mean, who naturally thinks industrial supplies is a great investment arena? Nobody, right?

I wanted to make sure I was creating maximum shareholder value, so I hired an investment banker. I asked him if he felt we were getting a fair market value, and he said, "Any time you want me to talk to some people and see if we can get some momentum . . . "

I said, "I'm not for sale, but if we come up in conversation and you think there's an interest, we would have no problem talking to a larger company about being acquired." When you're a publicly traded company, they call this strategy "seeking strategic alternatives," which is a fancy way of saying you're up for sale. Which we kind of were, but we also kind of weren't.

I told myself that if an amazing deal came through, I'd be interested, but I was just keeping my options open, which is smart strategy for any company, no matter what size.

CINDERELLA AT THE BALL

So I met with several companies. We began an off-the-record discussion with several industrial distribution companies; we also had a few serious meetings with big-time, well-known companies like W. W. Grainger and Sears. Yes, it was nice to flirt with the big companies and get flown around on private jets like Cinderella at the ball, but I didn't want the courtship to last forever. It's just not good for business.

In the end, none of the deals was a perfect fit, so I said, "Thanks, but no thanks. We're not for sale." Was I disappointed when those deals fell through? Not really. I was content to find the right decision for the business. If it wasn't meant to be, it wasn't meant to be.

I switched gears yet again.

I looked at our stock price. It had gone from eleven dollars all the way up to twenty-eight bucks. We had done such a great job explaining our business out of the gate that investors bought it and really seemed to love our story.

A few years passed, and we did some more acquisitions. Our annual growth rate dropped from 35 percent to only 20 percent. Then we missed one quarter, and our stock price dropped to fifteen bucks!

I was working like crazy trying to make it up, and one day, I looked around and asked myself, *What am I doing? It's clear everyone is hot for Internet stocks. Why am I killing myself trying to sell us to a mass audience?*

To make matters worse, I didn't even get to reap the full benefit of the deal!

My partners over at Summit were able to sell all of their Wilmar stock by 1998 for a great price, but not me. I was the "face of the company," so I had to be very wary of the selling rules and "optics" around selling company stock. The end result was I had to hold onto my stock long after Wilmar's stock price had peaked.

Was I bitter that my friends over at Summit sold their stock at a much higher price than me? Well, I didn't love it! But I took it in stride and learned my lesson. If you are ever considering partnering with someone, make sure your interests and your partners' interests are aligned, or you may end up getting much less than you bargained for!

THE HUNTED BECOMES
THE HUNTER

This is when I decided to take the company private with a group of high-profile private equity firms like Chase Capital Partners (now known as J.P. Morgan Chase), Parthenon Capital, and General Motors Pension Fund.

We sold at a valuation of $300 million.

We filed with the Securities and Exchange Commission, and by May 2000, we were back to being a privately held company—but I wasn't looking to stand pat. Instead, my goal was to start "looking to eat" in the form of acquiring more of our competitors.

Overnight, the hunted became the hunter—which put a gun in my hand and allowed me to go looking for some big game of my own. I loved the feeling of empowerment it gave me. Once again, I was back in control of the fate of my company. The control freak was happy again.

I thought all my troubles were over. I thought my privacy was back—no way! I went to my first board meeting, and I looked around, and there were twenty-five people around the table! How was this possible? We only had a seven-person board of directors.

You want to know how? Every private equity shop brought two people, the company brought four people, every bank had a person at the table, and the mezzanine debt holders had a person or two.

I thought to myself, *Here I am again. Pick your poison.*

I had mistakenly believed that by being private again, I wouldn't have to put up with annoying public shareholders anymore, but there I was, the CEO of a private company, with even more people to deal with. To quote Michael Corleone in *The Godfather*, "Just when I thought I was out, they pulled me back in."

The good news was "going private" turned out to be the right move for Wilmar. Even Jim Cramer, who you may know from CNBC's *Mad Money*, wrote a nice piece about us on TheStreet. com shortly after we went private. I even got an opportunity to meet Jim (who is a fellow Philly guy) at a Sixers game in 2000.

I remember he walked by my seats at halftime, and we started talking. Jim reiterated that Wilmar had made the right move. Man, that was music to my ears. I'm a big watcher of CNBC, so hearing Jim give his blessing gave me confidence that we were heading in the right direction. And confidence was exactly what I would need to tackle the new challenges that awaited me in the next chapter of my career.

I bring all this up because the real subject is the definition of success. What does success mean to you? Is it something measured purely in dollars? Is it getting the best table in the hottest restaurant, or courtside seats at the biggest games? Does it have to do with how you get along with your spouse and family?

Let's take a deeper dive into what success really means. That's the subject of the next chapter.

KEY TAKEAWAYS

- Never stop climbing. Keep raising your game.
- Tactical leadership means doing things right; strategic leadership means doing the right things.
- The best CEOs are always planning their next move. So should you.
- Have a plan and stick to it.
- Taking your company public means a ton of change for you—for better or for worse. Know all the pros and cons before taking the leap.
- Don't settle for your current success.
- Put your wisdom and experience to work to help grow your business.

CHAPTER 9

MASTERING THE ART
OF THE ACQUISITION

*When you're growing towards a peak, you need to work
harder than ever to find yourself another peak.*

—Bel Pesce, TED speaker and entrepreneur

ALL GOOD THINGS PASS.
PLAN FOR IT.

How do you define success? In sports, it's about winning
the championship. In Hollywood, it's about winning an Oscar.
And in politics, it's winning the next election. What does "all the
marbles" mean to you? Would you know what success looked
like if it landed in your lap?

Say you're kicking butt right now. What's your endgame?
I'm not future-tripping; now is the time to think about this
stuff. You need to understand that all TV series (no matter how
amazing) will be canceled one day, so how would you script the
perfect ending to your fairy tale? You better think about a third
act for your rags-to-riches story—or someone else will.

Maybe you are screaming, "But I never want it to end, Coach Green. I live to work. I'll stop when I'm dead!" That may be true. You may not stop till you drop, but what about your role in this business? How long will that last?

Is there another chapter in your career?

For many, the answer to this question is a resounding "no." A lot of entrepreneurs love their big idea so much, they'll shepherd their baby from cradle to grave. But if you want to see what else is out there for you in this big beautiful world, now is a good time to start thinking about a graceful exit strategy, on your terms.

81: SUCCESS CAN BE AN OPTICAL ILLUSION

Want to know a little secret? The closer you get to ultimate success, the further away it always seems. Maybe you, the entrepreneur, are creating the optical illusion. Maybe ambition is a sickness. But the last thing you want to do is let your ambition run amuck and burn out before you've taken care of your family.

You want to enjoy what you've worked so hard for, right?

Am I saying, "Be greedy?" Not at all, but if you can reduce your personal risk in your business, you might find there is another hill out there to climb. I attribute this urge to keep climbing to our entrepreneurial DNA. There is something inside all the great entrepreneurs that motivates them to keep looking to the horizon and striving for more.

Why am I talking about all this stuff?

These were the thoughts running through my mind.

Did I want to stick around for Wilmar's next chapter? I was still young. I wanted to take it to the next level in my life, but did that mean staying with the company for the duration—or did it mean cashing out and moving on to something else?

I looked around the industrial supplies market and realized there was nowhere else for us to go except up. Wilmar had to keep growing to reach the next rung. Did I even have the toolbox to do it?

Buying companies was a completely different animal that required a different skill set. I knew if I wanted my business to keep growing, I had to keep growing with it—so what did I do?

I took the challenge. I decided to stay and grow along with Wilmar. The business had to eat to survive, so I got busy improving myself. I worked my butt off to become good at deal making, acquisitions, negotiations, and corporate integrations. How did I transition to carnivore so smoothly?

It was by necessity. The market dictated it; I didn't follow any rules, because there weren't any. Despite what a lot of investment bankers and analytics people say, deal making is not a science or even a calculated gamble; it's more human than all that. Putting together a great deal takes a lot of elusive intangibles. It takes combining excellent information with preternatural people skills, courage, and the instincts to know when to strike and when to wait until you have a better position.

82: WHO WANTS IT THE LEAST, WINS

Every deal has its own dynamic, but here is one universal tip: the more leverage you have, the better it will turn out for you. It took me a while to learn this. As you well know, I was a reluctant carnivore. I was happy growing organically for eighteen years, but I made a strategic decision to sharpen my claws. Wilmar couldn't stay in the super middleweight division anymore. If we wanted to achieve the "ultimate" success, we had to push our way into the heavyweight class. We were on a mission! Cue the *Rocky* theme song.

So there I was, prowling the jungle with my newly acquired "eye of the tiger." At this point, Wilmar was considered a "tween" company, which (in hoops terms) meant we were too big to play the guard position and too small to bang with the "trees" down in the paint. We'd been filling up the box score for years, but Wilmar couldn't continue to grow if we kept playing small ball. It was time to big up if we wanted to keep trending up.

So I did. I wanted the championship so badly, I started acquiring companies, but that didn't mean I began acting like a jackass general manager. Bad free-agent signings can kill a good team! You have to be extremely smart; you have to do your homework. I'm not kidding when I say most free-agent signings are busts.

The first rule is, don't fall in love.

Never get so smitten you think you need to sign this free agent. "Take it or leave it" should be your state of mind. Think of buying companies like grocery shopping. Never do it when you're hungry, or you'll end up with buyer's remorse.

Sit out the feeding frenzies.

Don't get in bidding wars.

Never tip your hand.

Whether you actually want to buy something is beside the point. Feigning mild interest gives you the leverage in most negotiations. Sometimes, the other guy or gal is a cool customer, and you might end up in a stalemate—so I can't give you my secret to negotiating success—but I promise you, whoever wants it the least has the power.

It's been true since the beginning of time.

83: NEVER MAKE A DEAL WITH A GUN TO YOUR HEAD

How can you tell who has the leverage? If you're not sure, it's probably not you! If you start flirting with buying a company, you need to figure out if you are negotiating from a point of strength or weakness.

Don't be the guy or gal that needs the deal to go down.

If you are that guy or gal, the odds are good you're going to get screwed. I've been involved in many situations where I wanted to buy or sell something that turned out less than ideal. I know what the pressure feels like: it's up to you to make a deal, right? You gotta deliver!

Guys like Michael Jordan and Kobe Bryant thrive in crunch time, but "nailing daggers at the buzzer" is not what you should be concerned with. So don't put yourself in situations where you are down by ten points with a minute left in the game—and need to make a deal to save your business. Never let them see you sweat. Be boring. Be Gregg Popovich and the San Antonio Spurs. Be John Stockton and Karl Malone. Those guys rarely played hero ball because they were always ahead in crunch time, which meant they had the leverage when it mattered most. See what I'm saying here?

Here's an example where I felt like I had to play hero ball, and it could have turned out better. Looking back to when I was taking Wilmar private, I can see that I was mentally operating at a point of weakness. How so?

I was not happy. I still had 50 percent of my net worth in Wilmar stock, my chips were all out on the table, and I'll admit I was kind of scared. My stock wasn't performing as well as I wanted, so I felt there was some risk to the business going forward. I felt like I had to do a deal. I felt like I didn't have a choice, even though I really did—but I was so burned out, it felt like I had a gun to my head.

These are all very bad feelings to have.

It was a horrible position to be in; I thought I had no leverage. A prestigious group of private equity firms were offering me eighteen dollars a share (we eventually settled on eighteen and a quarter), which I felt was low. Why didn't I just tell them, "That's not high enough; I'm having fun running this company anyway. Call me when your offer is at twenty-one?"

Because I didn't have leverage, that's why.

Compare that to right now. If somebody came to me today and said, "I'm going to give you ten million bucks for LendingOne," I would say, "Come back in three to four years, because I'm going to be worth twenty times that!" But thirteen years ago? I had no leverage. I would've said, "Where do I sign?"

"Leverage is everything" is not just a business lesson. It's a life lesson, a love lesson, a marriage lesson—an everything lesson.

Never make a deal with a gun to your head, and you'll probably turn out okay in this world.

84: THE BEST DEALS ARE THE ONES YOU DON'T MAKE

This may sound like a mind-bender to a wheeler-dealer capitalist like you, but the best deals in life are the ones you don't make. I could spend the next few pages talking about deals I didn't do that would curl your toes. I would have been in trouble if I had completed any of them, which underscores my point: there are way more bad deals out there than good deals.

The deals where you can say, "I have leverage, and I'm going to pass" usually turn out okay. Sure, you could miss out on investing in some next big thing—but those don't come around very often. The good deals are rare. Some might look good on paper but are terrible in the integration and execution, while others are just bad ideas from the beginning (hello, AOL/Time Warner) and should have never, ever been done.

When Wilmar was public, there were shareholders and stock analysts who always wanted to know when we were doing the next deal. You know what I told them? "We are always looking at acquisition opportunities, but I'm not going to buy a business for the sake of buying one. You have to buy the right company."

That advice is still true today.

Say you invest twenty million dollars in a new company. Guess what? You could have invested that same $20 million in your own company and gotten a better ROI (return on investment). But investing in your own organic growth is boring, right? Acquiring a new company is exciting. Making a deal is fun! It's what gets people talking, so you're going to continue to get seduced by people who will ask you, "What about this deal?" Don't fall for their trap! Don't let anyone influence you into making a decision you don't want to.

The best deals are the ones you don't make.

85: KEEP YOUR BRAND GAME STRONG

I didn't get seduced (for the most part) when it came to Wilmar's acquisitions. I did my homework with my team before I integrated fifteen competitors into the Wilmar family from 1996 to 2001. The companies included: One Source Supply, Pier Angeli (my old nemesis), Sexauer, Trayco, Sun Valley, Gulf Coast, Supply Depot, Aaron Supply, Management Supply, Lindley, Kurzon Supply, AMS, ACE, Miniblind—and a big public company that sold the same products we did but in different markets, called Barnett, and its four subsidiaries: US Lock, Hardware Express, LeRan Copper, and Maintenance USA.

I could write an entire book about acquisitions. Each one had its own unique story, but here is one universal lesson you should never forget: the power of existing brands is strong. Make sure their customers and employees understand your endgame.

I tried to live by this lesson.

I rarely touched the new brands and kept each one separate from the rest of the business until the brand integration was safe. With the big acquisitions like Sexauer and Barnett, we already knew their brand was strong, so we didn't dare touch them.

Here are some other considerations when you're deciding whether to keep an acquired brand separate.

1. Capitalizing on Adjacent Markets—One of the first brands we kept separate was our first adjacent market acquisition; I paid eighty million for a company called Sexauer, which sold plumbing supplies to hospitals, nursing homes, and hotels. My logic was, if we kept the Sexauer brand in place, we could hit the ground running in this new market with a leader in the space. Which is exactly what we did, and it worked out well for us.

2. Leveraging Adjacent Markets—Another great reason not to chop a company's brand is if it reaches an adjacent market to yours. This is what happened when we bought Barnett. They were going through similar issues to what we were with a wavy stock price. Of course with all of the synergies, I saw the potential value in acquiring them. I knew Barnett's stock fluctuation had nothing to do with performance and everything to do with the fact that nobody wanted to invest in stodgy industrial distribution companies back in 2000. They were virtually selling our same product line, except they were primarily selling to contractors, remodeling guys, and hardware stores, which was a new (adjacent) market for us.

Would buying them make sense?

We started talking to the Barnett people. I was nervous about the deal since it was the biggest one we had ever proposed by far. Meanwhile, my CFO Bill Sanford, whom I'd hired in May 1999, was pushing it like crazy, but I kept pumping the brakes until I could see there were a lot of reasons why it made sense.

The biggest benefit to buying Barnett was massive integration synergies.

Here is a great example. Wilmar sold the same items as Barnett, right? So if we bought Barnett, we could increase the profit margins of both companies by getting lower costs of goods from our vendors, since we'd be buying more volume, combining our warehouses and back-end processing, while still maintaining separate brands.

Another big perk was that Barnett had just built brand-new office space in Florida and was already constructing a 300,000-square-foot distribution center in Nashville. I thought, *Man, if we owned those spaces, we could streamline our shipping routes. All of our vendors could ship their products to one central hub in Nashville, and we could turn around and ship them to our network of smaller local warehouses.* All of these benefits filled a big need, so we decided to do the deal.

BECOMING INTERLINE BRANDS

After the Barnett acquisition, Wilmar was now a $640 million annual revenue company. It was a real game changer. Acquiring their national distribution center was monumental.

After the deal was done, I looked around and realized we were finally in the heavyweight class. We had arrived. We got so big, we changed our corporate name from Wilmar Industries to Interline Brands.

Why did we do that? Hadn't we just chopped our brand? No.

Here is how it worked: We kept the Wilmar brand going since it was one of the largest companies selling to the multifamily market in the US with great brand recognition. We also left all the core brands we had acquired in place for all sales and marketing functions.

Interline was just the umbrella corporation that handled all the back-end business. Interline never touched a client, which allowed us to consolidate all our behind-the-scenes operations while never asking any of our clients to change who they did business with.

Sounds pretty smart, right?

It was for us, but what we did may not be right for your business. Perhaps your company's brand is so strong that any competitor you acquire would benefit from being fully integrated under your shingle. If you aren't sure what to do with an acquired company, remember why you wanted to buy it in the first place.

If a big part is that it already has a strong brand and a loyal clientele why throw away what you just bought?

86: LEARN FROM YOUR INTEGRATION MISTAKES

I don't want to sound like I am some branding integration guru. Let me tell you, I had to make some mistakes to get it right. My first big screw-up happened when I tried to integrate our first acquisition, One Source Supply. It was my first deal and I was inexperienced. I remember thinking we needed to squeeze all the possible synergies (on day one) out of the acquisition. Why? Because it would be a good IPO story. I thought, *What if we could do the transition over the weekend and hit the ground running?*

That sounded great, but in reality, I didn't give us enough time to do it properly. There was just too much change for the customer to do everything right. I couldn't help myself. I had delusions of grandeur.

Wilmar bought One Source on Thursday. On Friday night, we brought in a SWAT team from headquarters and converted their building to Wilmar. We changed all their parts numbers in their warehouse; we had our IT guys shut down their system and take over all of their computers.

By Monday morning, when One Source reopened for business, we were now "Wilmar, your One Source Supply."

It seemed like a smart move on paper. What went wrong?

Strategy and execution.

I guess it was my ego that compelled me to change One Source's brand, and it turns out, that was a big freaking deal! We didn't keep their brand pristine. When their customers heard our reps say, "Wilmar, Your One Source Supply," they replied, "Oh, you're Wilmar. I don't buy from you. I used to buy from One Source, but now I'm going to buy from someone else!"

They expressed their displeasure in no uncertain terms. I heard a lot of "Bill, what were you thinking?" comments from their customers.

When I saw what was happening, I admitted to my team and our new customers that the acquisition hadn't gone well out of the gate. I admitted the One Source customers were upset because we had made a lot of mistakes. I vowed to do better.

It was a tough lesson—and one I'll never forget.

In hindsight, the biggest problem with the One Source acquisition was not that I changed its name; the problem was that I did it too quickly. When you buy a company, you want to have synergies fast—but not too fast.

You have to make sure your timing is right.

87: NEW EMPLOYEES WILL ALWAYS BE SKEPTICAL

Angering our new customers wasn't all that went wrong with our first integration. I told you it was a teachable lesson! The One Source Supply integration was fraught with errors. The warehouse we thought we did a great job converting wasn't that great. There were also errors when it came to integrating employees, which is pretty common.

You should know that winning over the hearts and minds of new employees is always going to be one of the toughest challenges after an acquisition. It's only natural for new employees to feel loyal to the old regime. Even when they say they love you, it will take time for them to mean it.

Don't get your feelings hurt. Put yourself in their shoes.

I remember when I introduced myself to the One Source team, I put my arms around their number one sales guy and said, "Jessie, I bought this company because I wanted you." You know what Jessie said?

"Why didn't you call me?"

Jessie was skeptical of me (his new boss), and rightly so. I was screwing with his job security! I'd be upset, too.

The hardest thing I had to do during the One Source acquisition was lay off seventeen of its employees. I wanted to be empathetic, but I also had to be okay with people not liking me. No matter how amazing of a company you own, when you acquire a business, there are often redundancies, so layoffs are just part of the process.

In the end, I learned a lot from the One Source acquisition. I used to joke, "I took a ten-million-dollar company and grew it to eight!" because that is what happened in the short term. But in the long term, we recovered pretty quickly. To this day, Miami, which was One Source country, remains one of Wilmar's strongest markets.

So despite all the growing pains, the deal eventually worked.

88: DON'T LET YOUR EGO MAKE BUSINESS DECISIONS

Let me tell you about one more "integration fail" that was doomed before I even signed the deal. Remember when I told you about the time I acquired Pier Angeli? It was the company I dreamt of becoming when I was a kid.

Buying Pier Angeli was an amazing accomplishment, but it was not a great business investment. I let my ego get the best of me. Looking back, I shouldn't have made the deal; we paid too much. Yes, Pier Angeli had a great name nationally, so we were able to monetize some of the revenue spent on the acquisition, but not nearly enough.

I blame myself for getting into an imaginary pissing contest. It all started after Pier Angeli sued me for lifting material from its catalogues. Shortly after the lawsuit ended, I was in Chicago for the National Hardware Show—and guess who I ran into? My nemesis, Pete Pierangeli! He wouldn't even speak to me. Why all the animosity? Because we buried them.

But burying them wasn't enough. After the company sued me, I had to take it further. I was so intent on fulfilling my childhood dream (and shoving it in my dad's face), I made it my mission to own Pier Angeli. So I did.

Sure, it felt good to tell my dad about it . . . but after that?

It was a hollow victory that was a complete pain to integrate. Think about it: Pete Pierangeli Jr. came to work for us, so it was like trying to incorporate your sworn enemy into your inner circle. It just didn't work. I found out Pier Angeli had spent years brainwashing its salespeople to hate Wilmar, so we lost a lot of Pier Angeli's sales force when the announcement was made. There was no love lost between Wilmar and Pier Angeli—so why did I try to force it? Because of ego?

Don't follow my lead on this one. Forced marriages never work!

89: HAVE AN EXIT STRATEGY

Now we have come full circle, back to having an exit strategy—back to knowing when enough is enough. This question had percolated inside me for years. Then Interline became a $640 million company that had already acquired many of our competitors. I felt it was time to move on. The biggest reason was that I no longer had enough stake in the game to put my entire life into it—and I knew full commitment was the only way you can truly be a great CEO.

But here I was, still helming the Barnett integration and flying all over the country to make sure it went off right. It was a lot of work, but I was a good soldier who did a great job. And that's when I started to see the forest from the trees.

I remember thinking, *What else is there for me to do at Interline?* We had bought many of our competitors in the multifamily-apartment-building industry. Interline was now one of the largest industrial distribution businesses in the United States.

It was time for me to go. Barnett would be my last deal at Interline. Was the stress of integrating Barnett one of the things that pushed me into retirement?

Not really. Looking back, it was probably the events of September 11, 2001. In the aftermath of that tragedy, I remember thinking, *Life is so fragile.* I could have been in one of those towers or on one of those planes. I had business meetings in those buildings many times before. That's when it dawned on me: *I'm forty-three years old. I only have three million dollars of equity in Interline and have plenty of money in the bank. What am I doing here?*

I went home and talked about it with Amy. We both looked at where we were and said, "Why not go live the next chapter of our lives?"

Just like that, I said, "Enough is enough."

It was an emotional decision that was really hard for me to make. It actually took me a few tries before I resigned! No one but Amy believed I would really do it. But I knew this was the right thing to do for my family, the company, and myself.

I didn't just walk away. I agreed to be the company's "nonexecutive chairman" for the next three years. I wanted to make sure the transition was seamless, and it was. The company was eventually fine without me. I had hired Michael Grebe in November 1998 as executive vice president and promoted him in 2001 to be my successor CEO—so the company was in good hands.

I had had an amazing run, but I had taken my baby as far as I wanted to go. So I let her go. I stepped down as CEO of Wilmar/Interline Brands on my forty-third birthday, December 31, 2001, wearing a huge smile on my face . . .

Talk about exciting times—I could do anything I wanted. I had more money than I ever dreamed possible; I was still relatively young with a wonderful wife and great kids. Amy probably thought I was going to become the best husband ever and transform into a jovial retired guy, but that only lasted a couple of months.

Sorry, Amy.

I really did try to take it easy, but the life of leisure just wasn't for me. I can't help it. I guess I'm an antsy dude. I need to do something. I can't just sit around! What was I going to do next? Retire? C'mon, man. I wasn't done . . . not by a long shot.

I'm a scorer. And a scorer's gotta shoot.

Of course, if you're going to shoot, you better make sure you're aiming for the right basket. And that's what the next chapter is all about.

KEY TAKEAWAYS

- Would you recognize success if it landed in your lap?
- Make sure you have an exit strategy.
- Enjoy the fruits of your labors.
- Don't fall in love—don't get in bidding wars.
- Sometimes playing it cool will give you necessary leverage in negotiations.
- If you feel like you've got a gun to your head during negotiations, back away—you have no leverage in this situation.
- The power of existing brands is strong—keep that in mind during acquisitions.
- Things may be a little bumpy post-acquisition: expect it and give everyone time to adjust.

CHAPTER 10:

RETIREMENT? NOT SO FAST

The goal isn't more money.
The goal is living life on your terms.

—Chris Brogan, journalist

KEEPING MY DAD GAME STRONG

Ever thought about what your life would look like if all your dreams came true? I know what mine looked like after I achieved my ultimate goal: pretty much the same. But with fewer appointments. A lot fewer—I'm talking zero!

The morning after I resigned from Wilmar/Interline, I woke up and sat up in bed. It was the first day of a new year (January 1, 2002) and the first morning of the rest of my life. I had no alarm clock buzzing in my ear, no voicemails to check, no inbox full of emails; I had no customers calling, no employee issues, and no meetings to attend.

What was I going to do with myself?

In the whirlwind few months since I had decided to "hang 'em up" at Wilmar/Interline and move on from the only real job I'd ever known, I had reduced my financial risk and professional responsibilities to zero. Now all the pressure was truly off. The only obligations I had to anyone were to Amy and my three wonderful children: Allison (fourteen), Laura (twelve), and Adam (nine).

I know every dad says, "Gee, kids, if I didn't have to work all the time, what a great dad I would be." Well, now was my chance to prove it. Before I resigned, I had to find creative ways to spend quality time with the kids. Now I was able to really get involved.

What a gift.

So what did I do? What do you think I did? I got involved.

I dedicated myself to becoming an amazing husband and father. I grabbed my whistle and volunteered to coach all my kids' teams (Allison's Cherry Hill travel soccer and Maccabi teams, and Laura's and Adam's basketball teams).

When I wasn't coaching one of their games, I was playing "Geek Dad," running around snapping photos of them with my 35mm camera. It was a special time. I didn't miss a school function; I was home for dinner with the kids every night. For the first time ever, I could honestly say that I was completely present at the dinner table. It's amazing how clear your thinking can become when you are not distracted by the nonstop stress of work!

I was enjoying living in the moment.

I started doing triathlons again after a seven-year hiatus, which felt great. Meanwhile, Amy and I were focused on finishing up building our new beach home on the Jersey Shore and looking forward to spending our first summer there, especially since it would be the only time all year that all three of our kids would be away at the same time—thanks to summer camp. It was going to be our second honeymoon!

I was very happy.

I felt like I had won the life lottery. Everything was perfect. But as the days began to tick by, I was also extremely bored. Am I a bad person for admitting that? I hope not, but it's the truth.

Living a so-called "perfect life" can be boring. No one ever tells you that. I love my family more than anything on earth, but in the back of my mind, I kept hearing that little voice telling me, *A shooter's gotta score. A shooter's gotta score . . .*

SATISFYING MY SHOOTER'S MENTALITY

Even before I left Wilmar/Interline, I knew staying at home was not going to be an ideal situation for me. Sure, I loved the idea of being Super Husband and Mr. Mom, but in reality, I still felt that itch. You know that feeling, I'm sure; it's probably the same urge that inspired you to buy this book. Guess what? It never goes away.

I was at the pinnacle of my life and couldn't fully enjoy it. I was already itching to get back out in the business world and do something new. It didn't take me long to find logical reasons to get out of the house. I saw my kids didn't need me around 24/7 (they were in school), and neither did my wife! The only other things I had going on were trading my portfolio and building my beach house. Building it was exciting, but not an everyday job unless you were swinging a hammer.

I will admit, I got a little stir-crazy.

Enter my good buddy, Tom Meyer.

Tom is a fellow Camden Community College dropout who managed to make something of himself, just like me. He's been a good friend ever since I walked into his wealth management company back in 1989 with every cent I had ($20,000). He's been managing some of my money ever since. Our wives are also great friends, so one day during my semiretirement, he and his wife stopped by the house.

Tom took one look at what I was doing, or not doing, and said, "Bill, what you need is an office away from home," and he offered me one at his firm.

I thought, *I don't need an office away from home, but it would be someplace to go hang around and trade some of my stocks.*

So I said, "Why not?"

BOREDOM LEADS TO A
REBRANDING EFFORT

I talked about it with Amy. I assured her I wasn't coming out of retirement; I was just going to hang around the gym and put up a few shots.

Yeah, right. She knew me too well. She knew I wasn't ready to ride off into the sunset, but she okayed my going into Tom's office every day to trade my stocks as a part-time gig.

I thought being stuck at home was boring; I had no idea how boring the life of a day trader would be! Trading my portfolio was like watching paint dry. I had no control over anything and couldn't affect the outcome the way I was accustomed to. It was frustrating.

So after trading some stock every day, I would get bored, and my eyes would glaze over, then wander. I wasn't looking at other women around Tom's office, mind you; I was sizing up the business scenarios around me. I can't help it; my mind is wired that way.

I started examining Tom's office space like Kevin Spacey in *The Usual Suspects*—and the one thing that stuck out was the name of his company: Financial Architects. I remember thinking, *What does* Financial Architects *even mean?* It sounded small-time to me—except Tom's business wasn't that small; he was managing about $80 million in assets.

So one day, I casually asked him, "Why is your company called Financial Architects?"

Tom explained he inherited the name and the business from his grandfather.

I said, "No disrespect, but I think the name sounds like a mom-and-pop store. Think about the biggest financial services firms in the world. Goldman Sachs, Salomon Smith Barney, J.P. Morgan, Morgan Stanley—what do they all have in common?"

Tom said, "I don't know, but I bet you are going to tell me."

"They're all people's names, right? And you have a great last name! I think the name of your company should be something like Meyer Capital."

Tom said, "You may be right."

So I got an informal focus group together to test out his company name. Remember, I had nothing to do. After Tom saw the results, he finally agreed with me.

I said, "Great, I'll help you rebrand, but I'm going to need a budget." I knew this would be a sticking point.

Tom, God bless him, is one of the most spendthrift guys I know; he hates spending money. So I let him mull it over for a while. Then he came back to me and said, "Okay, I'll give you $10,000 to rebrand the business and create all the new documentation and marketing collateral."

I said, "C'mon, Tom, just ten grand? That isn't much."

Of course, he wouldn't budge. Luckily, I'd worked on shoestring budgets before—and again, I was bored out of my mind—so I agreed that, in exchange for my free office, I would lead the rebranding of his company with his $10,000 budget.

A few weeks later, I came up with his new name, Meyer Capital Group. Tom loved his new corporate identity.

I had a lot of experience rebranding acquired companies at Wilmar/Interline, so I made sure we didn't rush the Meyer Capital Group rebranding like we had with One Source Supply. We created beautiful new marketing collateral and announced the name change through a well-executed PR initiative, which made the transition seamless. All of Tom's existing clients were happy, and a whole bunch of new ones flocked to Meyer Capital Group like never before.

I remember looking at Tom, after it was clear the name change was a hit, and saying to him, "Now people are going to call in and say, 'I want to speak with Mr. Meyer . . .'"

Tom really loved that.

Looking back, that one simple rebranding effort has worked out great for his business. I don't know if you'll ever find yourself in the same "stale brand" position that Tom's business Financial Architects was in before its name change, but if you are holding on to an old brand because of legacy or loyalty to a past regime, or whatever, get with the times!

Rebranding a stale brand can do wonders for your business. Just look at Meyer Capital Group for proof. Maybe it's just a coincidence, but Tom has more than $900 million under management today. And yes, as I predicted—he now has new clients calling him who want to know what Mr. Meyer thinks! Better yet, his son Tom Meyer Jr., at age 23, just joined the firm, with his younger son Marc aspiring to join them after he finishes college. As Tom would say, "Now that's a beautiful thing."

GOING BACK TO GET THAT MONKEY OFF MY BACK

I was still searching for ways to fill my time, so I started my own bucket list out of morbid boredom one day. I noticed that, near the top of my bucket list was one big hairy monkey that had been on my back my entire life: Get your college degree.

I put down my pencil and said, "I'm going to do it." Real or imagined, I'd had that beast on my back my entire life. I wanted to cross that off my list.

Since I still had my dad duties, I couldn't stray far from home, so the first college I considered was Rutgers University. I wrote a letter to the dean of its business school, but didn't hear back, so I called up their registrar's office and found out I was too late to enroll for the upcoming semester.

I decided to go back to where it all began.

I drove over to my old "alma mater," Camden County College, which now had an annex in Cherry Hill, and registered for one class: English 2. A week later, I was in my first class. I was pretty excited to be a forty-three-year-old freshman.

I was on top of the world when I got home from class that day. I thought, *Okay, I'm really accomplishing something now!* Then the phone rang. It was the dean of Rutgers' business school—he got my letter and invited me to a meeting, so I went. The dean was a nice guy. He showed me around campus and laid out a path to getting the degree I'd always yearned to own.

He said I could enroll the following semester. It all sounded great; I was going to get my BA and then my master's. But then, Father Time gave me a wake-up call. I was struggling in my one English 2 class at Camden County College (CCC)!

This, I did not expect.

I mean, I have a pretty big ego, and this is community college here. But the struggle was real. I got a C on my first paper for my English 2 class. I was livid. I thought, *How did I get a C? I'm really working at this.* I vowed to work harder, which is what I did—but going back to school was not as easy as I had thought.

While I eventually did ace my one English 2 class at CCC, I decided not to pursue my academic career any further. Could I have become a great student if I had really dedicated myself to it? I think so, but I never gave myself a chance. I was always working on making money.

This time, I didn't try to fight my nature. Since it had taken that much effort to get one A, I didn't feel like I could take a full course load without it affecting my parenting duties. Instead, I became a guest professor at Rutgers for one day each year for the next four years. Meanwhile, I was back to the drawing board, still searching for that next mountain to climb in the business world.

No one said it was going to be easy.

90: WHEN ALL ELSE FAILS, LISTEN TO RESPECTED PEERS

At this point, I stopped fooling myself. I had thought I could stay away from the game and live out my days basking on the beach or shooting the breeze on the golf course. But who was I kidding? No one! With going back to school out of the picture, the Meyer Capital Group rebranding project was just the tip of the iceberg. I had to keep scratching that shooter's itch.

Instead of playing more golf, which (believe me) I tried, I started spending more time talking shop with my peers in an organization I had joined back in 1997 called the Young Presidents Organization (YPO). My involvement with YPO during my semiretirement was huge. It saved me.

Even though I was still on the sidelines, YPO let me apply my shooter's mentality to the world of business. I had to keep my head in the game somehow, and it helped me stay sharp.

I found out about YPO in 1997 through my two good friends Jeff Harrow and Sid Brown. I remember telling them I didn't have time to join, and you know what they told me? They said, "Bill, you don't have time *not* to join YPO."

Nearly twenty years later, YPO has been one of the biggest influences in my life. My YPO forum group, in particular, was pivotal during this transition period when I was looking for that next mountain to climb. What made it special?

YPO is a global network of CEOs and presidents with a mission of becoming better leaders through lifelong learning and idea exchange. The group has 24,000 members, but what makes it invaluable, at least to me, is my YPO forum group.

Those nine guys are like brothers to me.

I can say in all honesty that I trust them with my life. Everyone in my forum is sworn to confidentiality so you can bring up any issue—be it professional, personal, whatever—and you know it will stay in "the vault." I could get my nine forum guys on the phone right now and get honest feedback on anything.

I lean on them today just like I leaned on them back in 2002. We give each other great advice that would cost a fortune in consulting. These aren't just your average guys—they are all super smart and successful.

Jeff Harrow, who is in my forum, is like the older brother I never had. When I left Wilmar/Interline, Jeff had sold his startup travel agency to American Express and was already working on his new venture, so he knew what I was going through.

Robert Potamkin was another forum member who was a big help. Robert owns one of the largest car dealership groups in the United States. When I was going through the decision at Wilmar/Interline to either sell the company to a strategic buyer or sell my shares through the privatization (which I did), Robert spent hours on the phone with me helping me through this critical decision.

Do you want to know what these guys advised me to do back in 2002?

They said, "You have to get to know yourself, Bill. What makes you happy? If you ask us, we think you should keep looking for that next business challenge, but only you know what will make you happy."

They didn't want to put words in my mouth, but they knew I was a scorer and would never be happy just sitting around.

They were right.

I'm so glad I reached out to them during this time. I know it's hard for type A personalities to do it sometimes, but no human being is an island. If you have no idea where to turn next in life, seek out smart people who will give you good advice. Leverage your peers! I know the value of this kind of network; trust me. A good sounding board can help lead you out of the darkness . . .

It sure did for me.

91: KNOW YOURSELF TO PLEASE YOURSELF

I had my YPO forum brothers on my side cheering me on—but it didn't change the fact that I was still "unemployed." It was now the summer of 2002. All my buddies were working every day. No one I knew had retired yet. Remember that old saying, "It's lonely at the top?" or that old Sinatra song "Is That All There Is?" Not to sound ungrateful for all the blessings I have received in life, but I remember combing the beach by myself back in 2002 and thinking, *Man, that sure does ring true for me.*

I was wealthy, healthy, happy, and completely bored stiff.

The dog days of summer were getting to me. I was spending a lot of time in Longport hanging out at our newly constructed beach house with Amy. We were having a great second honeymoon; I couldn't ask for more in life.

Yet I was! I told you, I need the action!

So there I am, one day, on the beach with my close friend Sid Brown. He was one of the guys who introduced me to YPO. After graduating from Harvard Business School, Sid helped his father (Bernie) build his midsized trucking company into one of the largest trucking, logistics, and warehousing companies in the country, NFI Industries.

I had (and still have) a lot of respect for Sid, so I confided in him. I told him I was wandering aimlessly through the barren wasteland of retirement. Just then, Bernie, who happened to live in a high-rise building nearby, walked over and said, "Hey, Bill, what are you doing these days?"

I told him, "Nothing. I was thinking about going back to school, but . . . "

Bernie said, "Forget that. You've got to do something." This was coming from a seventy-eight-year-old guy, who even now, at ninety-two, still manages his own personal commercial real estate portfolio!

Sid followed up by saying, "I can't see how you could possibly retire, Bill. At our age, it's more than money; it's more than boredom. It's your identity. It is who you are."

I had never thought about it that way, but Sid and Bernie were spot on. I had to do something. Why?

Because it's who I am.

Sid and Bernie helped me realize something important about myself that day: doing business is a big part of my identity, a huge part. In many ways, it's who I am and what I was put on Earth to do. I wasn't ready to ride off into the sunset at forty-three. I was still a young man with a lot of great ideas, so I began working even harder to uncover my next big business idea.

I had already done everything I could in industrial distribution; it was time for a change, which I feel is a huge lesson for all of you out there. I might never be able to ace college Calculus 2, but I could still learn a few new business tricks! And that is so important when it comes to evolving your personal skill set. Just because you have a lot of success in one industry doesn't mean you have to stay there forever, people. Don't pigeonhole yourself: the world will try to do that for you, believe me.

The world certainly tried to pigeonhole me after my Wilmar/Interline days. People thought I was only a "business-to-business, plumbing, hardware, and electrical supplies" guy. They knew I could take a company public, but just like all of you who are reading this book, I knew I had more in me.

I wanted to do more than what was expected.

Maybe deep down, I didn't want to be known as just "the Wilmar guy."

Maybe I didn't want to be known as a one-trick pony.

Maybe that is what motivated me to keep scoring.

The bottom line is, it doesn't matter what motivates you to do it—you have to make a lifelong effort to keep remaking yourself if you want to stay above the rest of the scorers in this world.

Everybody likes a story that gets better over time—so make your life story interesting! Switch things up! I know what you're thinking: *Well, Bill, you had plenty of money. You could afford to take risks and do different things.*

And that is true. But it doesn't change the fact that once you stop evolving as a person, you start to stagnate, you get complacent, and you lose your edge.

I sure as hell didn't want to lose my edge—not at forty-three. Good old Dad probably thought I was nuts (I didn't ask him!), but I was ready to rock the boat once again. I pulled out my hunting rifle and went looking for big game. I decided I wanted to bag a midsized business. So I looked around. And I looked around . . . Then I looked around some more . . .

It took me a while to realize I didn't want to buy someone else's big business; I had just spent the past twenty-five years of my life building my own. I had no interest in throwing everything I had into a risky new project. So I looked smaller. There were problems there, too. How so?

I found that the smaller businesses were too small. For me, jumping back into a business that size would have felt like going back to 1987. In other words, there was not enough risk! So after doing a lot of research on both ends of the high-low risk spectrum, I determined that buying a business was off the table for me.

Now what?

I was back to square one.

WSG PARTNERS IS BORN

Then, serendipity struck. Sometimes, that's all you need.

It started one day in early 2003, when I got a call from my friend Charles Santoro. I met Charles when we were taking Wilmar public; at the time, he was the managing director of investment banking at Paine Webber. By now, he had started his own private equity firm, Sterling Investment Partners, one of the four firms involved in Wilmar's "go-private" deal.

He told me he was working on acquiring an 80 percent stake in a Philadelphia-based business, US Maintenance (USM), a rapidly growing facility maintenance company that provided retail chains with janitorial, landscaping, and snow removal services. I thought USM had a pretty cool one-stop-shop vendor management business model, so Charles asked me to be on USM's board of directors. He thought I would be a good mentor to the current CEO.

I was intrigued. I knew Charles was a smart guy, and I already had experience sitting on boards (my friends at Summit Partners had asked me to be on the board of one of their portfolio companies back in 1997).

So I thought about it. I trusted Charles. I thought, *Why not do it?*

Charles said I could also invest up to two million dollars in the deal alongside him if I wanted.

Just like that, Charles' offer gave me a big idea.

I thought, instead of investing two million with Charles' investment group, why not invest $500,000 of my own money into USM—then offer the other $1.5 million to people I knew? That way, instead of charging the standard 2 percent management fee (and 20 percent of the upside, known as the carried interest), I would do it for less than most private equity firms.

I would do it for a 1 percent management fee and 10 percent carried interest.

Man, I got all tingly just thinking about it. Was this my next big idea? I wasn't sure. It wasn't a revolutionary concept, but it sounded like a business model that just might suit my current needs to a tee.

I floated the idea to some of my inner circle. It didn't take long to convince my friends Sid Brown and Arnie Galman to invest $250,000 apiece. I also got a Philadelphia-based money management firm called CMS to invest another million dollars.

Had I stumbled onto my second business?

My mind raced with the possibilities. I knew a lot of investment bankers and private equity firms; I thought, why not make this my new mountain to climb? Just like that, I created WSG Partners, and we made our first investment into USM in August of 2003.

It had taken me more than a year and a half, but I was back, baby.

92: KILLING IT NOW DOESN'T MEAN YOU ALWAYS WILL

WSG Partners was my big new thing—and it was beautiful. Even Amy was happy I was out of the house again.

Now I just had to make it work.

Once we had our shingle up and running, I informed my friends at Summit Partners and a few other firms that I was available to sit on the boards of companies in which they were investing and would exchange my board services for the opportunity to co-invest alongside them, on the same terms as their investment.

Sounds pretty smart, right?

I told my investment banking friends the same thing. I had to convince them that letting me see the deals they were bringing to market would be worth their time. But I sold them on the fact that, with my background, I would attract some private equity firms to invest in their deals.

My contacts flocked to my proposal. I started flying all over, to New York, Chicago, and Boston, calling on private equity and investment banking firms to "ching up" some deals, as they say in the business.

Three years later, WSG Partners sold US Maintenance for seven and a quarter times our investment. Everybody loved Billy. That was a good one!

Looking back, it kind of spoiled me for the rest of them. I didn't know it then, but just because you have a big hit immediately doesn't mean you're going to strike gold every time out.

Private equity investing is a game of averages.

As they say, "Sometimes you eat the bear, and sometimes the bear eats you."

ONE-MAN BANDS NEVER GO FAR

So there I was, back at work again. Amy didn't love seeing me filling up the box score again, but she understood why I was doing it. I had to shoot! I didn't stop with USM; I was networking like crazy, going to private equity conferences, and doing everything I could to educate myself on my new business venture.

The next thing I knew, my phone was ringing off the hook, and I was looking at a lot of new deals. Like many ventures in life, you have to kiss a lot of pigs before you find any bacon—and I kissed a few! I kissed so many that it didn't take me long to realize that WSG Partners had the potential to be much more than a part-time job . . .

But I had promised my family I would not dive headfirst into WSG Partners like I had Wilmar, so I didn't let my urge to fill up the scorecard take over. I paced myself.

I couldn't keep up with all the investment memorandums I was receiving, so I hired my good friend Rick Swift to work with me. I knew Rick well; he was analytical and trustworthy. I could not pay him a lot at first, but he agreed to do the initial read-through on the proposals—and write one-page summaries for deals that could make sense for WSG Partners. It was a great working relationship. Now we just needed to start nailing more three-pointers to make all this effort worth our time.

NO PRODUCT WILL PLEASE EVERYONE

After Rick came on board, I received a call from John Svoboda of Svoboda Collins in Chicago. John told me about a hot new deal they had going in Portland, Oregon, to buy a company called Coffee Bean International (CBI), which roasted and packaged private label coffee for retailers like Target (for its Archer Farms brand coffee). They also supplied coffee to a lot of minimarts for companies like Chevron.

Coffee? What the heck did I know about roasting coffee?

The good news was, I knew John Svoboda and Michelle Collins when they were investment bankers at William Blair, and like Charles Santoro's Sterling Investment Partners, Svoboda Collins was also a small investor in the Wilmar privatization. So I trusted them and figured I'd invest alongside them. Why not?

Why not?

There were a bunch of reasons. I should have done more research, but I had an itchy trigger finger that needed to be scratched. So I invested—and this one bit me in the butt. There were all kinds of problem with this deal, man.

The biggest one was that CBI's CEO believed the false premise that CBI made the best coffee in the world. She'd act flabbergasted every time we didn't land a client. "Why didn't we get their business?" she'd ask. "We have the best coffee!"

I had to explain it to her: when it comes to matters of taste, you can't please everyone.

That is a lesson that applies to every industry in the world. There is no such thing as a 100 percent approval rating!

I remember telling her, "I'm no coffee connoisseur, but I have friends that swear by Dunkin' Donuts, and I have friends that swear by Starbucks. Everybody's got different tastes. We can't expect everyone to love us."

She just didn't get it—so to make a point, I walked into one of our CBI board meetings with a cup of Starbucks coffee in my hand. You can imagine that, at a coffee company, there was every kind of coffee we sold in the room, but I came in with a competitor's beverage in my hot little hand.

You should have seen the look on the CEO's face when she saw my cup! She asked me, "What are you doing with the Starbucks?"

I said, "I just like it better."

I don't think she liked that comment very much, but I was trying to prove a point. I think I did. But it didn't change anything.

The other big problem with CBI was its factory space. We thought the HQ was this hip, very productive distribution center when we toured it, but in reality, it was terrible. It looked cool, but it was not functional. It was behind the times.

It was just a big mistake. WSG Partners held CBI for three years, and it was painful all along the way. We eventually sold it to Farmer Brothers, but I took my first hit. I lost 40 percent of my investment. Ouch!

Like I said, you can't win them all in the private equity game. It's a risky business!

93: DO WHAT YOU LOVE, AND GOOD THINGS WILL HAPPEN

Even when you put up an air ball, you can't lose your confidence; you have to keep putting up good shots. I didn't back off. My next opportunity to score came when I heard about a deal to buy a company called Cigars International—they were a $20 million (per year) direct mail-order marketer of cigars.

I thought, *Now this is right up my alley. I love cigars. I love catalogues and direct mail . . . What's not to like here?*

I was passionate about this industry and the way they marketed themselves. I felt Svoboda Collins was a perfect partner for this deal, so they came onboard. I thought Michelle Collins was particularly well suited for it since she was a direct marketing guru who was already sitting on the board of CDW, one of the largest marketers of computers and tech products, and on the board of Coldwater Creek, which began as a direct-mail apparel retailer.

I was excited to sit on the board with Michelle; I thought she could teach me something about business-to-consumer direct marketing (and she did). I had done a lot of direct marketing at Wilmar, but it was always business-to-business.

This was a different animal, so I took the plunge with trusted partners into uncharted territory. I'd said I wanted to do something different, right?

So I did.

We bought 80 percent of Cigars International in July of 2004. Thirty-seven months later, we sold it for seven and a half times our money to Swedish Match, one of the largest cigar manufacturers in the world.

Were we just lucky or good on this deal? I didn't know, but this was our second big hit; we were doing great.

Looking back on the three investments we made in and around 2003 and 2004 (USM, CBI, and Cigars International), we lost 40 percent of our investment in CBI. The upside was, we made all of it back, and much more, with USM and Cigars International.

So there I was, a still semiretired dad, and I was two for three on my first private equity deals. I thought, *Not a bad shooting percentage for a guy who just got off the bench after nearly two years.*

I was happy again.

After those deals, I invested in six more companies. We had our share of winners and losers, but I'm proud to say that, overall, we boasted a 22.5 percent annual return on investment.

Not too shabby for a retirement job.

KEY TAKEAWAYS

- Getting ready to retire? Prepare for a whole new way of life that doesn't involve the boardroom.
- Avoid boredom by putting together a bucket list. Then start meeting those goals.
- Reach out and listen to your peers who have gone through this already.
- Don't be a one-trick pony—life in retirement can be your second act.
- Do what you love and everything else will fall into place.
- Recognize when your wants and desires should be attended to. Don't neglect yourself in the name of the company!
- You may want to go back to work because you're bored—make sure coming out of retirement is the best decision for you in the long term.

CHAPTER 11

ONE-TRICK PONY NO MORE

We make a living by what we get,
but we make a life by what we give.

—Winston Churchill

YOU CAN AGE IN REVERSE

So there I was, living my second life and loving every minute of it. I felt like I was aging in reverse. When most "retirees" were spending their days sipping umbrella drinks or playing shuffleboard, I was the forty-five-year-old dude on the beach who was looking to make deals 24/7.

Somehow, I'd convinced my family that I was semiretired while still playing a role in businesses that I was invested in. How did I pull it off? I promised Amy I wouldn't fall down on my family duties, that's how.

I went into my new Cherry Hill office every day while still doing all my Mr. Mom duties and being a "semisuper hubby" to my wife. It took me a couple of years, but I had found my sweet spot when it came to striking that elusive work-life balance. I thought I had it good when I was a bored retired guy on the beach. Now I had the best of both worlds.

I was one happy guy again.

In the private equity world, I was getting well known as an operating partner that could add value to any company, so I was in a good place. I could pick and choose my investments. I had the freedom to invest as much capital as I wanted to make a deal interesting, but not so much that I exposed myself to financial risk that could impact my lifestyle. I was working with private equity firms I liked and trusted. The entire thing was a delicate balancing act, but it was working.

I had pulled off another magic trick.

I was a "retired" guy (in disguise) that still had his business identity fully intact, just like Sid and Bernie suggested.

This was huge.

Not only was I maintaining my identity, but I was also adding to it. I was no longer a one-trick pony. With my private equity experience under my belt, I could honestly say that I was at least a two-trick horse now! That may not seem like a big deal to all of you who have been multitasking since birth, but it sure was to me.

PUTTING OUT FIRES ON THE USS *ARAMSCO*

By now, it was the end of 2004. I was sitting on the board of US Maintenance, Coffee Bean International, and Cigars International while meeting with investment banking and private equity firms about new deals.

This is when I allowed myself to get my head turned by one of the most interesting acquisitions I ever participated in. Don't be fooled: interesting doesn't always mean fun! And this one sure as heck wasn't. I didn't know what a real disaster looked like until I signed up for a tour of duty at a company called Aramsco, which is ironic since it was a company that sold products to clean up disasters.

My affair with Aramsco started when I met CEO Bill Kenworthy and his partner Dave Naylor, who together owned 60 percent of the company. Aramsco was conveniently headquartered in

Thorofare, New Jersey, which I loved, so I started to dig around on doing a potential deal.

On paper, Aramsco appeared to be right in my wheelhouse. Its business model was pretty similar to Wilmar's as far as sales, customer service, marketing, and distribution went, except it sold safety products and specialized in asbestos abatement, restoration products, and homeland security supplies.

In 2004, Aramsco took in $130 million in revenue and $11 million in earnings, which sounded healthy to me. Of the $130 million in sales, $72 million consisted of asbestos abatement products; $50 million of homeland security products; and $8 million of restoration products for hurricanes, floods, and oil spills.

Kenworthy pitched me hard. He said he didn't just want me to cobble together a group of investors to buy the company; he wanted me to help him maximize the company's valuation any way possible.

PUTTING THE DEAL TOGETHER

I thought about it and decided to help Kenworthy. As a reward for recruiting the investor groups, Bill said I could invest in Aramsco alongside whoever ended up buying the company. I said, "I'm in," so I called on a few of my investment banking relationships, and then I called Kelly Drake at William Blair, which did a lot of work with industrial distribution companies like Wilmar. Then I spread the word to my private equity firm friends and my good friend Joe Trustey, the managing partner at Summit Partners. I really liked Joe and Summit for this deal. I had already flirted with joining them for a number of deals, so I knew what they liked.

But I stayed neutral.

I was drumming up interest with a bunch of investment groups, but I did not align myself with any of them. I waited to see what firms showed serious interest in the process. At the end of a long process, it came down to two private equity firms. Both wanted me involved, so I was in a good position, no matter how it shook out.

Of course, when push came to shove, I helped Summit win the deal. We paid $82 million for 80 percent of Aramsco, which was 7.5 times the amount of their EBITDA (Earnings Before Interest, Taxes, Depreciation, and Amortization)! Summit Partners invested $38 million, while my investment group was in for $1 million (I threw in $550,000).

So there we all were, suddenly strapped with $43 million in debt, which was almost exactly four times Aramsco's annual earnings in a good year! How long would it take to earn back our investment? That was the $82 million question.

Maybe it was irrational exuberance, but we all really believed in the future of the company. Everyone was singing "Kum Ba Yah" when we signed the deal. Champagne was popped. Everything was great. We were ready to inflict some damage on our competition!

Little did we know what was in store for us—or the company.

SUCCESS HAS EVERYTHING TO DO WITH TIMING

I was named Aramsco's nonexecutive chairman in March of 2005. Since Summit and I owned 80 percent of the company, I started hanging around Kenworthy quite a bit. Bill and his guys were very interested in learning how I built a big distribution business, so I shared what knowledge I had on the subject.

The new Aramsco board was even paying me a small salary to mentor the current CEO, Kenworthy, which was unusual. They felt my Wilmar experience would help him, and it did— although I willingly admit our initial success had nothing to do with me, and everything to do with timing.

How could we have predicted that, a few months after we bought the company, Hurricane Katrina, the mother of all storms, would slam the Gulf Coast?

We couldn't.

Still, Aramsco responded to the disaster by knocking the cover off the ball. In a matter of days, we set up a temporary warehouse in New Orleans and were selling millions of dollars' worth of supplies to the Federal Emergency Management Agency

(FEMA) and private cleanup contractors. Our purchasing department cleaned manufacturers out of any disaster relief inventory we could get our hands on.

Katrina was such a massive storm it boosted sales for 2005 and a good chunk of 2006. We earned $160 million in sales that first year. I thought, *I guess we truly are in an emerging market that is here to stay.* Not only was Aramsco providing a much-needed service, we were making a profit doing so. Many experts agreed that the effects of global warming meant that natural disasters were unfortunately going to be a part of our future indefinitely.

Not quite.

The company prospered while natural disasters were hitting the country, but when things calmed down, guess what? No disasters. Sales were way down; the company was experiencing negative growth. Alarm bells were sounding all over the place, so I doubled down and started showing up at the Aramsco office a lot more often.

I wanted to understand what we could do to boost sales. The company had been doing $50 million in annual homeland security sales, but that figure had been dropping precipitously. What were we doing wrong?

The answer was nothing. And that was the problem.

94: NEVER INVEST IN AN UNPREDICTABLE MARKET

Aramsco seemed like a great investment, but the problem was the market was unpredictable. We didn't know what was going to happen. Our products had no expiration dates and were made to sit on shelves until someone needed to use them.

This was doubly a learning moment for me.

The first lesson that hit me was that one should never sell a product that doesn't need to be replaced. Think about that. If you've got to have a huge calamity happen for your business to turn a profit, you're in the wrong business. I didn't feel great working with a company that profited from disasters, but I justified it by saying we were helping people.

Still, I was in over my head. The company was in freefall, and somebody had to do something. I also needed to salvage my reputation. Summit had invested $38 million into Aramsco because Joe wanted to work with me again—and this was how I paid him back?

I kicked myself for being so naïve.

I agonized over this dumpster fire of a company.

"How did I miss this?" I wailed. "This is a stupid frickin' business model!"

Well, the reason I had missed it was that everyone had missed it. Not even the consultants we hired during our due diligence period predicted it. But you better believe it happened.

BACK IN THE CEO SADDLE AGAIN

There I was, organizing deck chairs on the *Titanic*, wishing I had never got involved in this one. It was mid-2006, so I was still involved in the other private equity deals I mentioned.

I had my semiretired hands full.

How was I spending most of my time?

Pulling my hair out over our problem child, Aramsco, of course. I became obsessed with finding a solution. I combed through its books like a madman, which revealed even more bad news. I remember calling Joe and saying, "It's worse than we thought. The Katrina cleanup is over, and homeland security sales are still tanking. This company is going sideways."

Joe urged me to put on my Superman cape. He said I should get back into day-to-day management and become Aramsco's new CEO, at least on an interim basis.

Replace Bill Kenworthy?

Joe was right. As much as I liked Kenworthy as a person, the truth was, the company was not professionally run at the time. Sure, everyone had put their best foot forward when they were meeting with all the private equity (PE) firms—but now? Their inexperience and lack of professional management skills showed. A lot of CEOs look like geniuses when they have great momentum, but not many look good when it's raining frogs from the sky.

It was raining frogs from the sky!

I remember telling Joe, "Make it worth my while, and I'll run the company." As soon as those words escaped from my mouth, I knew I wasn't kidding. Why would I give up my freewheeling, board-member-only lifestyle to run this business?

The first reason was obvious: to save my investment. I also did it because it was close to home, and I still had a burning passion to run a business again.

There, I admit it. I wanted to run a business again!

I started getting my itchy trigger finger watching the guys playing on the private equity courts; I can't tell you how many times I listened to some CEO talking at a board meeting and wanted to jump over the table and say, "Are you kidding me? C'mon! We can do better than this!"

I talked to Amy about it, and she gave me her blessing to try to save Aramsco. I think she just wanted me out of the house again. At the time, I thought I was riding in to save the day because they needed me. Now, I realize I did it for myself. I did it for my second life. I was a two-trick pony; could I possibly add another trick to my repertoire?

I had said I wanted to try new things, right?

BILLY, THE WARTIME CEO

Next thing I knew, September 5, 2006 rolled around, and I was back in the CEO saddle again, riding to the rescue to save what was left of the USS *Aramsco*. I walked into my new CEO office that first day feeling like a veteran three-point shooter brought off the bench to hit the game winning shot. I was excited!

Aramsco may have been a sinking ship, but it was my sinking ship.

I loved the pressure of having to come through in crunch time. The company needed emergency surgery—was I the guy to do it? Did I still have my shooter's touch? All I knew was, I had to reengineer Aramsco's business model, or we were crashing into the mountain.

No pressure, right?

We had to cut costs, so I took a closer look at all of Aramsco's end markets. How could I make the company more efficient?

The more I dug, the more my stomach churned—we were in trouble. Big trouble.

I called Joe after being CEO for three days. "It's worse than we thought," I said. "We're on track to do $7 million in earnings, not $10 million. We're in for a shit show!"

The business was in a death spiral.

I remember thinking, *I didn't sign up for this. I'm not a turnaround guy.* That's a different skill set—to go in like a mercenary and cut costs and fire people. That's not me. The only mass firing I had ever orchestrated had been the time I laid off those seventeen people at One Source!

But I didn't shy away from the challenge. I sucked it up.

I put on my army helmet, picked up my rifle, and got my hands bloody. Just like when I was chasing down primo spots at the flea markets back when I was a teenager, I did what I had to do.

I became a "wartime CEO" and started slashing. I contradicted one of my key principles, which was "You can't cost cut yourself to profitability." Why? I had no choice.

I became the bad guy to 235 employees. I trimmed the fat, froze wages, and renegotiated virtually every product vendor deal possible. When the dust settled, the cost-cutting and renegotiations were very helpful.

But not helpful enough.

95: IF YOU'RE GOING THE WRONG WAY, TURN AROUND

It didn't matter how much fat we trimmed; Aramsco was still on life support. Our overall business model no longer added up (post-Katrina). Our bread and butter were hurricane and flood prevention and asbestos removal—and I could see that every single one of those events was unpredictable or obsolete.

What do I mean?

You can't predict when disasters happen. And all of the asbestos removal buildings would be abated eventually, so guess what? One day soon, we wouldn't have any homeland security or asbestos cleanup business anymore.

I felt a twinge of panic. Two of our three end markets would soon be in ruins. I had to think bigger, or we were going to go full Hindenburg all over the East Coast. After I banged my head against the wall a while, it finally dawned on me how to save the company. To build a business that was predictable and stable, we needed to start thinking about disaster events as windfalls.

We couldn't count on them anymore.

I remember pulling my team into a meeting and saying, "Look, there's a whole other side of this business that we should explore. Aramsco can't just sit around waiting for terrorist attacks or natural disasters—we also sell to restoration contractors, right?" It wasn't a huge piece of the existing business, but it looked a heck of a lot more reliable than the "rain dance" portion of our offering.

What if we focused on targeting them?

My idea raised some eyebrows.

I explained, "Restoration contractors will always have water heaters bursting, pipes breaking, and roofs caving in from rainstorms. They're reliable customers. Why not target them instead of focusing on unreliable disaster prevention?"

I can't remember how long it took, but I sold them.

We reengineered the company and went after the restoration contractors, guns blazin'. Some people questioned the move, but you know what? It helped turn the business around. Did I feel that same rush of exhilaration after the big win?

Not really. I felt more relief than exhilaration on this one.

I knew I might have won the battle, but not the war.

TURNING THE SINKING SHIP AROUND

Don't get me wrong; I was happy that I had helped develop a strategy that turned Aramsco's sinking ship around. I was proud we had stopped the bleeding. But we weren't safe yet.

Fast-forward to a year later, and our restoration contractor business was doing well, but not well enough to offset the homeland security losses. I could still make it rain when I needed to, but I'm no miracle worker. I couldn't change the fact that Aramsco was a commodity business where you had to be cheapest to market. That is a very tough business model to grow.

I always say, "Get them on price; keep them on service." But Aramsco had a hard time doing that.

So after nearly two years as CEO, I saw my future if I stayed still. We were heading into the Great Recession of 2008. No construction projects were being done, so our asbestos abatement business was bottoming out as well.

It was clear Aramsco was going to be a different business going forward.

I was not ready to dig in for the long haul.

THE SILVER LINING IS ALWAYS THE PEOPLE

Do you want to know what the bright spot of the entire Aramsco deal was? It wasn't professionalizing the company or adding to my CEO game; the bright spot involved the people I worked with who made the whole fire drill of an experience worthwhile.

I want to give a big shout out to Rich Salerno, a first-year associate at Summit Partners when we first met in 2005. I'd just taken over as CEO of Aramsco, and Rich was and still is a brilliant young man who had just graduated at the top of his class from Boston College.

For the first few months I was CEO, Summit was nice enough to let Rich do some work for us. Rich was just twenty-six at the time, but I could see he did it all extremely well, be it analysis, financials, or projections. He planned to go to Harvard Business School, but in early 2007, Rich told me he wanted to stay and "help me turn this ship around."

I was furious. I remember asking him, "Who gives up the chance to go to one of the best and the most prestigious business schools in the world?"

But Rich was adamant. He said he'd learn more working for me than by going to Harvard, which was flattering but not true. I eventually gave in and hired Rich to be our vice president of corporate development.

Rich was an awesome employee. He helped me in every facet of the business. Remember how important it is to hire smart and hardworking people? Well, it really paid off for me with him.

Here's the kicker: After almost two years of working with Rich, I convinced Summit that it was time for me to step down and Rich should be named the new CEO.

Joe at Summit asked, "How in the hell could a twenty-eight-year-old run this company?"

I convinced Joe that Rich was the right person for the job. I wasn't doing anyone a solid here; Rich deserved the opportunity. I informed Summit I would stay on as nonexecutive chairman and help Rich with the transition, but not on a daily basis. It was settled.

After a two-year tour of duty, I resigned my CEO post with a smile on my face. I had never planned on staying long; it was all part of my master plan.

It was the right move.

Aramsco had acquired another business and more debt by the time I left it in 2009. Sales were at $125 million with $7.5 million in earnings, which was not terrible given the significant loss of much of the homeland security sales. Through all the lean times, Summit and I had somehow successfully written down our investment by 50 percent. We were hoping that, with the company's new direction and Rich running the day-to-day business, we would eventually be able to sell the company, pay off our debt, and get some of our investment back.

We eventually sold it to another PE firm in July 2013 for nearly double what it was worth a few years before. None of this would have been possible without Rich's excellent stewardship of it. He did a great job for four years. Instead of losing our butts, we made a 3 percent annualized return on our investment. That's not bad when you think about what we would have earned if our money had been in the stock market during that time.

Today, Aramsco is still kicking. Last year, it racked up more than $250 million in sales, with higher profits than ever before. Its homeland security division sold $3 million, down from $50 million. The company has grown by expanding its other lines of business, with restoration contractors accounting for a large portion of the growth.

Talk about a 180-degree turnaround of a business model.

THE SMART ADAPT

In the end, when all the fires were finally put out, the entire Aramsco fiasco drilled one big lesson into my head that all you entrepreneurs should file away.

Remember Lesson #12, because it never stops being true: "You can kid others, but don't kid yourself."

If your golden goose starts laying rotten eggs overnight, be straight with the person in the mirror and assess the situation objectively. If you determine that your golden goose is defective, then trust your analysis and say, "Okay, it's not working. Now what?"

If you realize you are going the wrong way, turn around immediately. Don't delay another second.

This rule applies not only to business but also to every single facet of life. Life is all about trial and error. We all make mistakes. We all go the wrong way. The smart ones make adjustments on the fly while the "less smart" follow the rest of the charging buffalo, who are so busy running blindly at a vague goal, they don't see the oncoming cliff.

Don't be part of the herd: lead the herd.

MY VENTURE INTO VC WATERS

This old silverback gorilla was proving he could nail three-pointers all over the private equity court—but PE was only a small part of the investment landscape. There were a lot of other games in town.

Before I took over as CEO of Aramsco, my network was bringing me dozens of PE deals, which was great, but then a few people started to suggest that I invest in venture capital (VC) deals. I had never invested in a startup before.

What's the difference between PE and VC investments? Good question.

VC firms mostly invest in startups or early-stage businesses with high growth potential, while PE firms usually invest in existing businesses that are already turning some kind of profit. Startups were really interesting, but clearly riskier. I remember thinking, *Should I stick my neck out for any of these deals?* The possibility of scoring big got the attention of my shooter's mentality.

I gave a bunch of VC deals some serious thought and decided, yes, I wanted to try something completely different. How hard could it be? I had no idea, but I was about to find out.

I let my network know that I was open to hearing some venture capital pitches. Not long after I floated the idea, I got a call to meet with the Herzog family in Brooklyn. The Herzogs were a family well known for owning a company called Royal Wine, the largest manufacturer of kosher wine in the world.

I thought, *Wine? I love wine. Just not kosher wine!*

I met with the Herzogs anyway.

I'LL SAY IT AGAIN: SWEAT EVERYTHING!

Turns out, the Herzogs weren't interested in adding to their wine business. They wanted to start a liquor company called Mystique Brands, which manufactured ready-made cosmos and apple martinis.

My co-investor and good buddy Sid Brown, a PE firm called Enhanced Capital Partners, and I thought ready-made cocktails were a great idea, so we invested $5 million to help the Herzogs launch the business.

As you know, we got the color wrong, so the drinks didn't look like cosmos or apple martinis—we didn't "sweat everything" on that one. But the biggest mistake happened immediately, and it had nothing to do with color.

We hired the wrong CEO to run the company, and it doomed us. That first hire is so important for any startup. When you airball that decision, you're hamstringing your company from the start.

And that is how I felt working with Mystique—hamstrung.

I don't know if anyone could have saved this business, but I feel like strong leadership would have helped. I take partial blame. I should have been all over our first CEO, but I wasn't. I thought he knew what he was doing—but the guy couldn't control costs. He spent way too much money on marketing.

The only positive memory I have from this investment was, after we replaced our CEO, we were given the exclusive distributor rights to Pierre Ferrand cognac, which was pretty cool. Cognac had become a very popular drink with the young crowd, and we thought we had a product that would help us recoup our lost investment from the martinis.

It didn't pan out, but the fun part was that we had an endorsement contract with Snoop Dogg, which made the entire experience more entertaining. While I was losing my shirt, I got to take my girls and wife to see a Snoop Dogg concert where we got to hang out backstage and were treated like VIPs. My kids loved this investment.

Me? Not so much.

Mystique could have had a hundred Snoop Doggs hawking our products, and we were still done! The nail in the coffin was that the cost to launch a new alcohol brand was way higher than what everyone involved was willing to invest. I still think it's an amazing product idea if somebody can execute it right—but in the end, you have to be okay with losing your shirt on any deal.

Otherwise, step away from the PE/VC tables: those games of risks are not for you.

KEY TAKEAWAYS

- You can be happy and productive in retirement if you plan it right.
- Unpredictable markets are bad investments.
- Know when you're heading in the wrong direction and be willing to change course to avoid disaster.
- Some investments may be poor business decisions, but you may learn something valuable from the experience nevertheless.
- Keep sweating all the details, no matter how small.

CHAPTER 12

THE CRESTAR STORY: NEVER STOP PIVOTING

The secret of change is to focus all your energy not on fighting the old, but on building the new.

—Socrates

SHOOTING 'TIL MY ARM FELL OFF

My second life as a private equity guy was going great; I could have kept shooting forever. It felt awesome to hear the net swish again, but after a few years of lighting up the private equity scoreboard, I asked myself, how much longer did I want to do this? Was this still my passion?

I liked hitting shots, but watching the ball go through the net was like watching paint dry. There was a lot of waiting. You'd make an investment, sit on a board of directors to help out, and wait for your investment to bear fruit (or not).

I thought, *Some current income would be nice.* So I started to wonder, *Could this two-trick pony do something else? How many tricks could I learn? What was the world record for the most eclectic business career?*

Whatever it was, I wanted to beat it.

I'm kidding. I wasn't interested in becoming "the most interesting man in the world" like that guy on the Dos Equis commercials—but I also knew that I didn't want to spend the rest of my career shooting at one net. I let my eye wander again. Hey, you only live once, right?

I was officially still in the private equity game but unofficially looking around for a new business opportunity. Given the recent downturn in home prices, I thought buying foreclosed homes and flipping them could be an interesting business to get into. Did I know anybody in that world?

I remembered a couple of guys at my country club had pitched me on the tax lien business a few years ago. Tax liens? Ugh, anything with the word *tax* made me queasy. All I knew about it was you could earn 18 percent interest on your investment, and if the property owner didn't pay it back, you could foreclose on his or her home. Foreclosures were supposedly "rare," but I didn't like the sound of throwing people out of their homes. I told the guys at the country club that I'd think about it, which was my nice way of saying, "I pass."

Fast-forward to February 2008, and I decide to call up those same two guys to discuss buying their tax lien foreclosures. They were two good guys (both named David) that I had known socially for years. They weren't budding financial wizards like Rich Salerno, but they had been running their own tax lien side business for the past five years called CCTS, Camden County Tax Service.

I told them I was playing around with the idea of starting a home fix/flip business. I said I thought flipping foreclosed homes could be a good investment idea, given the recent housing bubble collapse.

They replied, "Why buy already foreclosed homes when you can invest in our tax lien business and get foreclosed properties for much less?" The Davids explained they were looking to grow their business. They'd only bought tax liens in southern New Jersey at this point, and they needed to raise capital.

I asked if they were working with an investment banker. They weren't, so I introduced them to an investment banker friend in Philadelphia who helped the Davids put their investment memorandum together. They sent me the PowerPoint a few months later. It was pretty impressive.

Seeing it all explained professionally with a banker's help really helped me grasp the profitability potential. I told them, "It looked good, but I'm still not investing with you guys."

Why the heck not?

96: YOU'RE NEVER OLD ENOUGH TO STOP DOING HOMEWORK

I wasn't charging into unknown territory on this one.

Sure, I liked the potential, but I wanted to do due diligence and learn more about the market first. At the time, I was still the CEO of Aramsco (and on the board of several other companies I was invested in), so I was pretty busy. Nevertheless, I decided to learn all I could about the tax lien business in my spare time.

This is a great life lesson. It doesn't matter how much of a hotshot you think you are—you're going nowhere fast if you stop doing your homework. Even if you think you're already an expert in your chosen field, you are never too old to learn new things. Adding to your game is an essential part of being alive. Give it a shot, and you will be amazed to learn how much you don't know—so stay curious.

Personally, I became a human sponge. I got an awesome tan that summer because I was reading tax lien books like a son of a gun. But books weren't all I absorbed. I met with a few attorneys that specialized in tax lien foreclosures and called on numerous other tax lien companies (posing as an investor). I wanted to gather as much real-world information as I could on the tax lien business, so I also hired a guy recommended by one of the attorneys to attend a few of the auctions in New Jersey and buy some tax liens for me under my directions to see how the process worked.

Don't tell anybody, but I also peeked in on a few (incognito). What did I learn?

GETTING A TASTE OF TAX LIEN AUCTIONS

I found out the auctions were bonkers, man.

In many states, they're done 100 percent online, but not in New Jersey, where I was poking around. In New Jersey, they were done 100 percent in person at the town courthouse or municipal hall. The process was very primitive, which explains why you had to jump through so many hoops to get in on the game.

I'm not here to dump on my home state, so I will say this as nicely as I can. New Jersey's auction system was archaically devised for optimal inefficiency. In other words, it was twenty years behind the times.

Nothing was streamlined; it was pure chaos.

Another thing I learned was that tax liens were super granular. There were minutiae to learn in every facet of the business—from performing property due diligence to the auction itself, all the way to servicing the tax lien. If you jump into this business, you'd better know your cities, neighborhoods, and homes like the back of your hand (like a good real estate agent does), or you're going to get burned.

I didn't want to get burned.

So after experiencing my first real taste of the crazy auction process, I was convinced there was no way in hell I was going to try to build a tax lien business from the ground up. Too much risk. I also just didn't have the granular knowledge to do it myself. The smart move would be to partner with someone who did, which didn't sit well with me.

Why?

You know me well enough to know I don't like not knowing stuff. Maybe it was my ego talking, but I didn't like being an amateur in anything, so I studied even more. By November, I felt like I was informed enough to circle back with the Davids, who told me they were still looking for funding.

They asked me to invest once again. I said, "C'mon, guys, I'm not that type of investor. Give it a rest!" But they wouldn't take "no" for an answer. They kept recruiting me, hard. I still wasn't convinced that going into business with these guys was a good idea, but their enthusiasm wore me down. I said, "Let's talk about doing a deal together."

What finally convinced me I could thrive in this wild and woolly environment?

First, I stopped focusing on the foreclosures and started looking at the bigger picture. I knew property taxes were primary sources of revenue for most communities—so by purchasing tax liens on unpaid properties, I would be helping municipalities by giving them some current revenue in place of the IOU note the homeowner left them.

See how my mind works? I convinced myself I was doing some good! Cities needed revenue to fund critical public services like police and fire departments, public education systems, and municipal salaries, right?

I also figured my involvement would help taxpayers. If municipalities had to replace delinquent taxpayer money themselves without selling off the liens, then guess what? Taxpayers who did pay on time would have to pay more to help float the delinquencies.

But the biggest factor that convinced me to jump in was that I felt my track record of building effective processes into businesses would give me a competitive advantage in this arena. Call me brazen, call me cocky—but with the fall in real estate prices and a looming recession on the way, I felt I could get a good risk-adjusted return on my investment.

I would turn out to be right on both counts—at least for a little while.

CCTS CAPITAL IS BORN

With my confidence high, I jumped into a new game with both feet. I told the Davids, "Okay, you sold me. Let's get into bed together. I think I can add a lot of value to your business." They were ecstatic.

They asked me how much "action" I needed to make it interesting. If you know anything about me, you know I'm not going to do anything small. Did you think I was going to keep penny-anteing my way into the game? No way. To make it worth my time, I agreed to invest up to $10 million. I thought it would be a safe investment if we used my $10 million to raise another $40 million in bank debt.

We hammered out our roles. Since I ponied up all the $10 million myself, I now owned 100 percent of the company, which we rebranded from CCTS to CCTS Capital. I became the chairman, and the Davids ran the day-to-day operations. We all agreed the Davids could earn their way into a 25 percent ownership stake apiece once I got back an 8 percent return on my investment. They call that earning "sweat equity."

We signed the deal December 1, 2008. I bought CCTS's intellectual property (not the liens the Davids already owned).

I was all tingly with possibility. Was this deal going to soar— or crash and burn? That is why they play the games!

I went home and told Amy the news. She asked if I was unretiring for good.

I said, "No, my darling; this is just a hobby away from my family time."

For some reason, she bought it! Or she pretended to. God bless her, Amy knew it would make me happy

EVOLVING INTO CRESTAR CAPITAL

We launched CCTS Capital on December 1, 2008. A few months later, everything was going according to plan, except that, given the collapse of housing and world financial markets, we found out getting bank debt for this "eclectic" asset class was becoming virtually impossible!

Another problem was that, in February 2009, just two months into my new business, the media reported that one of our competitors, an institutional tax lien buyer, was under investigation by the Department of Justice for tax lien auction bid-rigging, better known as collusion, which is a violation of the Sherman Antitrust Act.

Yuck! I wanted no part of that, and I told my team as much. Even though all my employees had signed my standard code of ethics policy, I ended my business relationship with both Davids after seven months. No offense to those guys, but I didn't want any part of a business that could be exposed to any potential legal problems, let alone felonies. I also knew this business needed an infusion of professional management if we were ever going to grow according to my plan.

By July of 2009, I had left my day-to-day CEO responsibilities at Aramsco and was working like a madman on building a new tax lien acquisition and servicing team from the ground up. I was back in the CEO saddle again, but this time, I owned 100 percent of the company. With the Davids out of the picture, I wanted a fresh identity for the new business.

At the time, I thought the name CCTS meant something to tax collectors, so at first, I rebranded the company to Crestar Capital Tax Service to keep the CCTS intact. It didn't take long for me to realize a name meant absolutely nothing in the tax lien world! So I simplified the name to Crestar Capital, which was just vague-sounding enough that it left me open to invest in other kinds of business opportunities in the future.

This time, the name stuck.

THE WORLD LEARNS OUR LITTLE SECRET

It took a little time, but we finally got a bank to finance my new venture, and Crestar Capital was off! A year into the new business, I was asked to join the National Tax Lien Association's (NTLA's) board of directors, which I did. I served for the next five years. As you know, I didn't want to just know a lot about the business; I wanted to become as much of an expert as I could.

One thing it didn't take an expert to notice was the market was getting a lot more crowded. When I got in the tax lien business, most buyers were small or regional. There were a few institutional buyers like M. D. Sass and Mooring Financial—but the biggest player in the industry by far was J.P. Morgan through its Plymouth Park financial subsidiary.

A year later, in the wake of high unemployment and the housing market crash, the rest of the world had caught wind of our hot new business opportunity. The news spread incredibly rapidly.

Over the next few years, big players started pouring a ton of money into tax liens. An auction that had once attracted ten bidders (half institutional buyers and half mom-and-pop buyers) now attracted fifty people, and they were all big-time institutional types!

Our little secret was ours no more.

A lot of hedge funds were also now in the business. Want more proof that the tax lien business is deader than dead? I went to an NTLA meeting last year, and there was this speaker who asked the audience, "Stand up if you've been in the business for more than ten years." Eight guys stood up in a room of 150!

Then he said, "If you've been in this business one year, stand up."

The whole room stood up.

It wasn't just that demand for homes had increased—there were fewer foreclosed houses to choose from. Four times the money was now chasing half the supply of homes! In 2010, there was $1.5 billion in tax liens sold in the state of Florida alone. Fast-forward to 2014, and only $750 million in tax liens were sold in Florida, with a lot more bidders.

Watching the air come out of this so-called "hot market" so fast, I realized tax liens were a nice place to invest when the going was good, but not a sustainable business at the current volumes and profitability levels.

That said, overall, Crestar Capital went on to be pretty successful. By 2015, we had purchased $300 million in tax liens (45,000 liens) in five states. At our peak, we had $80 million in tax liens in our portfolio at once. Even though we scaled ourselves down after the market peaked, we made a 15 percent annualized return on our equity investment.

Not a bad return for a self-taught amateur.

IN SEARCH OF MY NEXT BIG IDEA

I sold Crestar Capital's tax lien portfolio in 2015 to a public company that they later securitized. The market had peaked. I was pretty much done. I've kept a hand in the game by keeping Crestar Capital going, even today. Who knows? Maybe I will jump back into it when the conditions improve, but for now, I'm on the sidelines.

Like I said, it has to be interesting for Coach Green to take off his whistle and get involved.

97: KEEP BUILDING OFF WHAT YOU KNOW

Let's back up a bit to January of 2012. My tax lien business was still maximizing its potential, but I could see what would happen. It wouldn't last forever, so I started to think, *What could I do next that would turn my head—and keep it turned?*

A lot of people in my high-tops might have switched gears again, but I had put a lot of blood, sweat, and tears into becoming . . . maybe not an expert, but at least a player in the tax lien arena. I didn't want to waste that experience, so I started brainstorming how I could parlay my tax lien experience into yet another business. Who would have thought my next big idea would come from watching television?

I'm serious. A business idea came to me while I was sitting in my home office watching CNBC's *Squawk Box* talk up single-family rental housing as a good investment. I remember thinking, *That would be one way to parlay my tax lien knowledge.*

So I made a note of it.

Two weeks later, I was watching *Squawk Box* again, and Warren Buffett came on. The anchor, Becky Quick, asked him, "What is your number one investment idea for 2012?" Warren replied, "Single-family rental housing." Becky asked, "Why aren't you in the business yourself?" Warren replied, "Because I can't buy a hundred thousand of them. My business is so big that, unless it could be a multibillion business, we just can't do it."

When I heard Warren's seal of approval, I said, "Okay, now you've got my attention." Why? First, I respect Warren Buffett's business acumen. Second, I felt my experience underwriting tax liens and acquiring foreclosed homes would give me an edge up on my competitors and (hopefully) make getting involved in single-family rental housing a very profitable endeavor.

The edge factor was huge. As you know, I have no interest in getting involved in any new business opportunity unless I have some kind of edge, so this looked good!

BATTLING THE BIG TIME FOR MARKET DENSITY

Why did I think I had a leg up in the single-family rental world?

I already owned real estate that I was foreclosing at cheap prices! So instead of just flipping them, I thought, *Why don't I renovate them and make them into single-family rental housing?*

This idea had legs . . . I didn't wait to get it up and running. I quickly formed a new business, Crestar Homes, and suddenly, I was a landlord.

I wasn't expecting this plot twist.

From that point on, we employed a multipronged strategy when evaluating homes. Remember Lesson #79: "Have a dual business strategy?" I'm telling you, it works. Now we didn't have all of our eggs in one basket.

Now we had options with every property we foreclosed on. We could flip the house, fix and flip, or fix to rent—depending on what was best. I wanted to get Crestar Homes in the best position to succeed in the current climate, so I decided that fix to rent was how we preferred to do business, as long as the home was in a safe area.

That is how we operated for the next three years.

Looking back, I'm not going to call Crestar Homes an enormous hit or a huge failure. Overall, I flipped 300 homes and owned 150 single-family rental homes. I still think single-family rentals is a great business if you're a big institutional buyer that can buy a bunch of properties in specific markets. But I didn't have that kind of financial backing, so I just couldn't get enough density in a given market.

I still believe that single-family rental housing is here to stay, regardless of how good the economy gets—but it just wasn't for me. Crestar Homes didn't give me the return I needed to make it worth my time. I was not interested in running a business with gross annual sales of $800,000!

I slowly pulled the rip cord. When one of my tenants did not renew a lease, I sold the home instead of finding a new tenant. It was time to pivot again.

There I was, pretty much out of the tax lien and single-family rental housing business. I was still a young man, relatively speaking, but when I looked up at the scoreboard, I felt like the shot clock was running down on my career. I was pivoting around like Kobe Bryant in the post looking for that perfect angle. I wasn't going to let the clock run out on my second life without draining a few more shots. A shooter's gotta score, right?

I started to think about how I could pivot off what I knew, yet again.

SAILING OFF INTO THE SUNSET? YOU'VE GOT THE WRONG GUY!

This is the part of the story when a normal person might have sailed off into the sunset and lived happily ever after, but not this crazy guy.

Sure, I could have retired to the beach in Boca Raton, started writing my memoirs, or joined a few corporate boards and been pretty happy doing it, but something inside me wouldn't let me hang my jersey from the rafters just yet. Even after I had had successful runs in pretty much all of my post-Wilmar businesses, I looked in the mirror and thought, *I'm not retiring. I don't want to sit around playing shuffleboard all day; I hate Bermuda shorts and white shoes!*

So I plotted my next move.

The tax lien business and Crestar Homes were still going great when I began flirting with a new investment opportunity in the fall of 2013. It all started when a friend of mine suggested I look into these two peer-to-peer (P2P) lending companies called Lending Club and Prosper. They initially interested me because of their unique business model. They loaned money like banks, yet they had no brick-and-mortar establishment. Their business was all done online. They didn't even provide the money for the loans; their users did!

How does that work? These companies function a lot like the crowdsourcing sites Kickstarter, GoFundMe, or Indiegogo. All they do is match lenders with borrowers. Let's say you get a $5,000 loan from one of these companies. Instead of one person owning your loan, there could be twenty people that owned a portion of it.

DIVING INTO CRESTAR LOAN FUND

They call this sort of thing marketplace lending or crowdfunding today. It's a hot market and has been since the 2008 financial crisis when a lot of people who could not get a bank loan turned to marketplace lending companies for help.

Lenders today enjoy using companies like Prosper and Lending Club, because they can buy a fraction of a loan and earn interest that is charged to the borrower minus a 1 percent servicing fee for the use of the platform. Borrowers who use these companies can get a fast and easy personal loan for their business, home improvements, or debt consolidation.

Lending money on one of these sites sounds promising, right?

I thought so. So I tested the waters; I invested $10,000 apiece at Lending Club and Prosper. I focused on buying thirty-six-month loans, which historically paid off in twenty-two months. I was having so much fun doing it, I decided to create a Crestar company that only did marketplace lending.

I called that company Crestar Loan Fund.

In the two and a half years Crestar Loan Fund was in business, we acquired over $32 million in consumer loans through Lending Club and Prosper as well as small business loans through two other companies, OnDeck and Funding Circle.

TO BE OR NOT TO BE INSTITUTIONAL

I thought my new "side business" was going pretty well. I was getting a nice return on investment. But you know me. I'm always pushing it. I thought, *Could business be going even better?* To make this worth my time, I hoped so. That's why six months into my new venture, I became an "institutional buyer" for Prosper. It was cool being a single investor who could buy into this asset class like large hedge funds or companies like BlackRock, the world's largest asset manager.

But I noticed the downside of being institutional was that you had to buy the whole loan versus a fraction of it. Banks would not lend money to buy fractional loans! Man, this was an amazing educational experience for me.

I was learning a lot and having fun doing it, but after two years, I realized I wasn't quite getting quite the action I desired. My investment never produced the midteens ROI (return on investment) I hoped it would. It did produce a return comparable to other asset classes—like the stock market or bonds—so what the heck was I complaining about?

I guess I knew, deep down, that marketplace lending was a nice place to park some cash, but since interest rates were inevitably going up, I didn't want to have a loan portfolio with locked-in rates that could compress my margins.

I said to myself, *Life's too short. This is not the best use of my time.* I suspended all new loan purchases from all platforms in early 2016.

98: IS IT A TRADE OR A BUSINESS?

After I finished my time with Crestar Loan Fund, I realized why it was not a sustainable business. It was not a business at all! Just like the tax lien business, marketplace lending really operated more like a trade.

A business is when you have a value proposition that brings something unique to the table, which attracts people to buy your products and invest in your company, right? A trade, on the other hand, is an action that performs a function that anybody can learn to do, like giving out a loan or making a stock trade.

The Crestar Loan Fund business was clearly a trade for me. I didn't have any customers. I was the only investor. I was making a return, but I wasn't helping my business. Crestar Loan Fund was actually benefitting Prosper's and Lending Club's business.

I'd have to own my own platform to truly call what I was doing a business, and I wasn't ready to hang my hat on a trade. But you better believe I took what I learned from this "trade" and applied it to my next "real" business. I knew I may not be raining threes all over the court like I once had, but there was no way I was done looking for another great shot.

PIVOTING INTO REAL ESTATE FINANCING

As I mentioned, while Crestar Loan Fund was going on, I still had my tax lien business and Crestar Homes running. I'm a multitasker; what can I say?

For my Crestar Homes portfolio, I was working with a few new entrants in the real estate finance business to acquire some debt on my fix-and-flip and single-family rental homes. After attempting to borrow money from these companies, which were all backed by huge hedge funds, I realized their loan processes were completely unorganized and not user-friendly.

Remember, banks don't typically lend money to buy distressed properties. Even if I waited for my properties to be renovated (and I had $100 million in my portfolio of properties), I couldn't get institutional lender financing at reasonable rates.

There is a niche lending business called hard money lending, but most of these lenders are mom-and-pop establishments that do not last. Even if they had achieved some scale, they weren't deploying technology and offering outstanding customer service.

I thought, *Could someone do this better?*

There was my pivot, on an industry I knew: real estate financing. It was familiar enough that I was confident I could do it, but new enough that it would be a "new trick" to learn. The good news was, no one appeared to be rushing to fill this void in the market.

I said to myself, *Why not me?* I took the plunge based simply on my belief that I could do it better. I didn't know how I was going to pull it off, but I put my mind to solving this puzzle.

I asked myself, *What have I learned about the real estate financing process that I could do better than the competition?*

99: BUILD NEW BUSINESSES OFF
WHAT YOU'VE LEARNED

Do you see what I just did there?

I just said to myself, *I'm going to start a new business by pivoting off what I know.* I'll say it again, this is huge! I pivoted my way into new businesses again and again throughout my career. Why do this? You never want to be part of a business where you can't bring something special to the table.

If I could not stand out in the crowd, I kept pivoting. It doesn't matter how great of a shooter you think you are, don't settle for an off-balance jumper with some defender's hands in your face. Keep pivoting until you find an open shot.

Once I decided I wanted to enter the real estate finance business, I thought about what skills I could bring to the table that would make me qualified to succeed. I wrote down a list of all my skills that I thought could help me.

Want to know what they were?

1. I knew how to value a property through my tax lien business and fix-and-flip and rental housing business.
2. I understood consumer credit through my experience with P2P/marketplace lending.
3. I understood rehab budgets from doing home renovations as well as my Wilmar/Interline days.
4. I knew I could bring customer-centric focus to the value proposition.
5. I knew what a great online platform looked like, one that would differentiate us in the marketplace and improve the borrowers' online experience.

When I added it all up, I realized my tax lien and fix-and-flip experience taught me how to underwrite real estate. I also knew how to underwrite borrowers after my two years in marketplace lending, so I combined those skills and the ones listed above to start a new real estate finance company that underwrites both.

Why build my own real estate finance business?

I thought it was a sustainable business that would flourish

in most economies and be a great risk-adjusted return on my investment. I felt I was uniquely positioned after my time with the Crestar Group of Companies to start a private real estate business that focused on fix-and-flip as well as fix-to-rent investors.

I told Amy all about my latest brilliant idea, and she yawned and said, "Whatever. You go." So I took off to start another company out of a good idea and a lot of ambition! I had no idea how I was going to do it, but I was euphoric. Why? I had this great idea. You know what that feels like, right? It's like you have this secret that you can't wait to show the world.

That is how I felt about this opportunity.

I'LL SAY IT AGAIN: BE A SECOND-MOVER PIONEER

With all the businesses I had going on (like my tax lien business and Crestar Homes), I knew I needed to hire a strong chief operating officer (COO) to help me spearhead the launch of my new real estate finance business.

I had already known Matt Neisser for eight years when I brought him on to help me start the company. He was a really smart real estate guy who had just gotten his MBA from Columbia.

We named our real estate finance business Crestar Funding.

Matt and I began outlining what we thought would be the right service offering and technology for the business. Crestar Funding started as a balance sheet lender, which meant we took loans on our balance sheet and owned them until they were paid off.

On December 1, 2014, we originated our first loan. I felt pretty good about being a balance sheet lender until we noticed some of our competitors were either selling their loans to institutions or crowdfunding the loans. I thought, *Wait a minute . . . You mean I have options when it comes to building our business's balance sheet?*

I started talking with a friend who was knowledgeable about marketplace lending. When I told him what we were doing, he asked, "Why are you a balance sheet lender? Would you rather own the gold or the gold mine?"

I thought, *Wow, that's really a great statement.* All of the highest-valued marketplace lending companies were not holding loans on their balance sheets. Why should we?

After that conversation, Matt and I pivoted off our original idea and became a company that originated loans and then sold them to hedge funds, just like our biggest competitor, Lending Home. And it's worked out great so far. This is still our business model today!

If you see your competition is doing something better than you are—don't let them run circles around you. Take action! I'm not saying to dabble in corporate espionage, but find out why they are beating you. Copy as much as you legally can from their winning blueprint, and then execute better than they do. You will be using their own weapons against them!

I'm telling you—become a second-mover pioneer.

WHY SO HIGH ON REAL ESTATE FINANCE?

A lot of people ask, "Why are you so excited about real estate finance?" Going in, I knew this business was going to be incredibly scalable, given the market dynamics, and that has proven to be true.

Another factor that gets me giddy when I think about the future is that the investor/lending side of the real estate finance business is still super fragmented. There are a zillion people that do fix-and-flip today.

Did you know that, in 2015, forty billion dollars' worth of homes were flipped in the United States? It's true. The US housing stock is currently worth fifteen trillion dollars. Fifteen percent of all the homes sold in the United States become single-family rental homes, and $2 trillion of US homes are already owned by investors who own fewer than ten properties.

If you want to talk potential, put a pencil to some of these figures. These people are our target customers. I told you, it's a huge market.

Amazingly, when we started Crestar Funding, no other online lender out there seemed to be employing a high level of customer service—or at least not high enough for my standards. It also seemed that only a small amount of the new entrants into the market were deploying any type of borrower-focused technology.

Now can you see why the dynamics around this had me incredibly intrigued?

CRESTAR FUNDING BECOMES LENDINGONE

After Matt and I launched Crestar Funding, it became clear this was going to be bigger than just an investment for Bill Green's portfolio. Here's why:

- By December 2014, we had issued our first loan.
- By the first half of 2015, we had originated $4 million in loans.
- By the second half of 2015, we had the industry's best proprietary technology.
- In 2015, we originated $25 million in fix-and-flip loans. And in 2016, as I write this, we will eclipse the $100 million dollar mark in loans originated since inception.

When we saw how big this business could be, Matt and I decided to create an identity for the business away from Crestar, just in case we wanted to bring in additional investors or "seek additional strategic financing alternatives," which as you know, is Wall Street speak for selling or going public!

That's how excited I am about this business. It could be that big.

It took a while to find a great name, but by November of 2015, we had rebranded our company LendingOne. I really feel like it's a business where I can use my expertise to do something different. Our thinking is that, by infusing a superior customer service culture into our people, our process, and our technology, we will differentiate ourselves from our competition. And we have so far.

LendingOne functions just like Uber, the biggest private taxi company in the world. Uber doesn't own a taxi, and we don't own any of our loans! I think our tagline sums us up nicely: "Reinventing private real estate lending through technology, process, and experience . . . "

Boom.

The irony is, if LendingOne had stayed a balance sheet lender, we'd be profitable now. Why? Because you get all the interest on the principal plus the origination points charged to the borrowers! When you sell the loans, all you get is the origination points and a servicing fee from the loan buyers.

Ah, well. The upside for me is I that will be able to grow LendingOne to be much larger than I could using my own money, which is what I really love about this business.

CRESTAR REAL ESTATE INCOME FUND

Despite LendingOne's rosy outlook, I stayed awake at night thinking about what could possibly screw it up. I went over all the what-ifs again and again—and found a possible hole in our offering.

We needed a contingency plan in case the hedge funds stopped buying our loans for some reason, like market volatility or due to their own capital constraints. If that ever happened, we'd need a backup outlet for our loans, or we would be screwed.

I wasn't going to let that happen, so I created Crestar Real Estate Income Fund, which buys one-year, fix-and-flip loans from LendingOne as well as a few of our competitors. Now, LendingOne does not have to sell its loans to hedge funds.

Once we put a little debt onto our Fund's balance sheet, we should be able to offer our Crestar Real Estate Income Fund investors a 15 percent return on investment. Stay tuned! I feel like it's a nice little alternative profit arm for our business, with a high-risk adjusted return. I'm telling you, when you find a great idea, create as many profit arms as you can, and milk that cow dry.

100: UNIQUE BUSINESS MODELS HAVE BRIGHT FUTURES

I'm trying to be cautiously optimistic when talking about LendingOne, but I am wildly excited about it. However, I've learned from past experience that you never know how the environment can change overnight.

But, as I write this book, I believe LendingOne is doing a great job filling a void in the real estate finance market. There are not a lot of fintech companies out there that can boast our unique offering. And no bank out there can match what we do!

We provide short-term loans to real estate investors who usually fix and flip a home in less than a year. Banks typically don't lend money to buy distressed real estate, and they certainly can't close on a loan from application to closing in ten days like LendingOne can. So we feel like we have a real advantage over traditional banks when it comes to serving this niche market of customers.

LendingOne is not the least expensive source of capital. Our interest rates are higher than banks', due to the short-term nature of our loans and the fast turnaround needed to receive the funds. Nevertheless, we're still a better option for most real estate fix-and-flip investors.

Our fix-and-flip loans are interest only and are only due when the investor sells the home. We call this our bridge loan.

We also offer term loans for buy-and-hold investors through our trademarked loan product we call our RentalOne loan. All of our rental loans are thirty-year amortization just like a conventional home mortgage. We offer a 5/1 and a 7/1 adjustable rate mortgage (the interest rate is fixed for five and seven years respectively and then adjustable for the remainder of the mortgage), but our most popular term loan is the thirty-year fixed rate.

I'm trying to wipe the smile off of my face while I'm talking up LendingOne, but it's hard! I mean, what's not to like, right? Down the road, I believe LendingOne can become a one-billion-dollar-a-year originator of real estate loans.

SURROUND YOURSELF WITH SMART PEOPLE

With our offering and website off and running, I made one final strategic move to help ensure LendingOne could max out its potential. I asked a really smart and extremely skilled advisor named Richard Vague to help me with strategy and top-level decisions. He's one of my closest friends, a YPO forum mate, and has been one of my advisors for the past few years.

Before LendingOne, Richard had never expressed any interest in investing in any of my businesses. But when he heard about this one, it piqued his interest, so he asked me if he could become an investor in the company.

So what did I do? I sold him a 10 percent stake in LendingOne. Why is Richard's input so valuable?

He was the co-founder of two major credit card companies, so he knows the credit business. He is also one of the smartest business guys I know. Remember Lesson #41: "Surround yourself with winners?"

That one never goes out of style. Just having Richard as a sounding board has been a huge asset. He is a true "reputation ally" that does nothing but bolster our corporate image. Having someone of Richard's caliber on my team is one of the best business decisions I've ever made.

I also asked two other friends to be on LendingOne's Advisory Board: Stan Middleman, the founder and CEO of one of the top ten mortgage originator companies in the United States, and Bill Cohane, who managed Wachovia's Real Estate Capital Markets United States REPO business.

What do all of these guys have in common? They have skills that complete me. And you can never have too many smart people working for you.

101: NOT EVERY DREAM COMES TRUE, AND THAT'S OKAY

Now that I have pumped you up to put down this book and go out there and follow your dream of starting your own amazing business, I want to share one final lesson with you that I learned five years ago.

To quote the Rolling Stones: "You can't always get what you want. But if you try sometimes, you just might find you get what you need."

Those lyrics hit home when I think about "the one that got away." What am I talking about? You know basketball was the most important thing in my life when I was a kid, right? Making money was second. Girls were third.

But the problem was, my genetics weren't helping me differentiate myself in the New Jersey high school basketball player market. I stopped growing at fourteen. Being generously 5'7" and slow, I didn't have a realistic shot to make my high school basketball team. But I never gave up my passion.

I remember the first time my parents scraped up enough money to send me to the Philadelphia 76ers Boys Camp in Medford, New Jersey. It was only ten miles from home; I was twelve and awestruck. Hal Greer and Billy Cunningham, two then current 76ers who are both now in the NBA Hall of Fame, taught me how to shoot. Billy nicknamed me "Turtle" because I was so slow. But I was tenacious; I kept working at it. When the two-week camp ended, I won MIP (Most Improved Player). I was in hoops heaven.

Fast-forward twenty-five years, and guess how I rewarded myself after I sold 55 percent of Wilmar to Summit Partners? I bought courtside Sixers season tickets, of course.

I was in hoops heaven again.

Then early 2011 came around, and something almost magical happened that would have been the cherry on top of my career. I was working on being part of an investment group to buy the Philadelphia 76ers.

We got so close.

Comcast (who owned the team) had tried to put the Sixers up for sale back in 2006, but it never happened, so I thought they were fishing for a sucker this time around. Still. I couldn't help myself. I was passionately interested in "my team," so I did some digging around.

Then an investment banker who specialized in sports team sales got wind of my interest. He called me up and told me he had an out-of-town group of investors interested in buying the 76ers alongside a local group of Philadelphia investors. This investment group already owned a professional sports franchise, and since they were all out of town, they were looking for a lead Philadelphia investor to be the face of the Sixers franchise.

Now, I don't want to sound like I'm the biggest 76ers fan on earth here, but I thought I fit that description—so I threw my hat in the ring.

Next thing I knew, I was sitting in the Sixers stadium offices, meeting with ownership executives. Our entire ownership group offered to pay $300 million for the team (minus the stadium, which Comcast would continue to own) with a significant amount of prearranged financing from the NBA.

The way the NBA works is, even though a group of investors can buy a team, one person has to be financially accountable for the group and has to invest a minimum of $35 million of his or her own money.

That figure was slightly past my financial capabilities, but I was willing to invest $10 million of my own money and give up all my other day-to-day business interests to become part of the team's executive management, assuming that I would be named CEO.

What did I know about running a sports team? Absolutely nothing. But I was confident that with my lifelong passion for the game of basketball plus my business knowledge, I could learn how to run one very quickly.

YOU CAN'T SINK ALL YOUR SHOTS IN LIFE

It was a roller-coaster ride for the next five months waiting for an answer.

Would my ultimate dream come true? There were days when I thought I was going to be the next CEO of the Philadelphia 76ers and many others where I was sure my dream was dead.

In the end, I wasn't that guy, and we weren't that investment group. Even when the deal got too rich for my initial investment group's blood, I didn't give up. I scrambled to find another group of investors and (specifically) one investor that would write the $35 million check.

All that effort was to no avail. In July, Comcast announced the team would be sold to another investment group. My lifelong dream was crushed into a million tiny pieces. Sure, I was (privately) despondent for a while, but I think it all worked out for the best in the end.

I didn't get what I wanted. But I got what I needed.

Some dreams don't come true, and that's okay.

That is what I want to share with you. Sometimes, you don't get what you want in this life, but you just might find that you get what you need. If you have a grand idea for a new business that you have determined is just too much for you to swallow— see if you can downsize your dream into something a little more manageable. I'm not saying to give up on your dream entirely. No way. Always be pivoting. But be smart about it.

I've found that some dreams (like being an astronaut or the owner and CEO of your favorite NBA team) are better left inside the mind of a child. Now that some time has passed, I'm thinking maybe it's better to just be a fan. The last thing I'd want to do is screw up the team I love and leave them worse off than when I found them, which (ahem) is exactly what has happened with the current ownership group.

C'mon Sixers, get it together already.

KEY TAKEAWAYS

- Always do your homework before heading into uncharted territory.
- In search of the next big idea? Build off your existing body of knowledge, and you'll learn the fine art of pivoting.
- Take every shot, but know you might not make them all—and that's OK.
- Some dreams will not become reality.
- When will your next big idea strike? Who knows, but be receptive to new ideas in new places.

CHAPTER 13

NOW IT'S YOUR TIME TO SHINE

Thinking good thoughts is not enough. Doing good deeds is not enough. Seeing others follow your good examples is enough.

—Douglas Horton, clergyman and academic leader

TIME FLIES WHEN YOU'RE LIVING YOUR DREAM

Where has the time gone? I can't believe it's been more than forty years since I set up my first flea market table way back in May of 1976, which started me on the sometimes unbelievable, oftentimes fantastic journey that I just shared with you. They say "time flies when you're having fun" for a reason, because it's so true! Looking back, it feels like my life has been one big blur of hard work, but I will tell you, I sure had a lot of fun doing it.

It's truly been a fulfilling blast, just like writing this book has been for me. I still have a lot of shots to sink, but I hope you have enjoyed reading about my ride from fledgling entrepreneur to successful CEO as much as I did living it.

Do you want to know what inspired me to write this book?

It was good old Dad, believe it or not. When Marty was diagnosed with Alzheimer's disease a few years ago, it really hit me hard. This rock of a stubborn old man whom I still love dearly was suddenly deteriorating before my eyes. Once the disease got hold of him, I noticed Dad no longer remembered much about the good old early days of Wilmar, which blew my mind.

How could someone forget such an integral part of his very existence?

It scared me. I won't lie.

I went home and talked to Amy. Could this happen to me too? Is Alzheimer's genetic? I found out that it was. I looked at Amy. " . . . I think I need to write down my story," I said, "just in case." And I'm so glad I did. This book isn't a complete account of my business career, but I feel like it's a fun and informative glimpse inside my head that I hope all my kids and grandkids will enjoy.

YOU'VE GOT WHAT IT TAKES TO WIN

I don't want to sound like we are both at the end of the journey here. I'm only fifty-seven years old. Who knows what tomorrow holds for both of us? If you ask me, I think our futures are pretty bright. I'm not just trying to pump you up; I'm serious.

Is it trite to say, "You remind me of me a little bit?"

It's true. You may not be some "grown-up kid" from New Jersey, obsessed with business and basketball—but you're not all that different from me. I definitely would have read this kind of book!

Clearly, you are an ambitious person who is serious about wanting to start your own business. You are also task-oriented, because you didn't put the book down until you were finished. This may sound like no big deal—but those are great traits to have if you want to make it in business.

I know, because I have them too.

BELIEVE IN THE POWER OF YOU

I really believe that, with those traits in your toolbox, you can do anything you set your mind to—so get to work already. Hone in on that big idea of yours, and when you finally have a plan that's worth risking it all to achieve, I feel confident you're going to "nail that shot." Coach Green believes in you.

So keep driving to the paint. Take the rock coast to coast if you must, like Dr. J! Never take your foot off the gas. And when you hit a roadblock (and believe me, you will), let your unbending belief in yourself fuel you to keep pressing on. I don't want to sound like motivational guru Tony Robbins, but you have to "believe in the power of you" (as much as I did myself) if you want to achieve your dream.

Are you up for the challenge? No one wins a championship by giving it his or her "almost best." You have to give it your all, and then some! My dream is that you will take what I have taught you and go start your own business that becomes bigger than any of my businesses. My dream is that you will become a "second-mover pioneer" and make a business that already exists even better. Whatever you do, I want you to do it with passion and do it with all your heart.

That, my friend, is a recipe for greatness.

FIND A WAY TO GIVE SOMETHING BACK

Want to know the real secret to happiness? It has nothing to do with power, prestige, or making money. If you ask me, it's showing your gratitude by giving something back. That is what life is all about.

People that give back are the happiest people.

I'm not saying that because I'm a religious man (I'm not). But I am humble enough to realize I have been blessed in many, many ways. Yes, I had a big dream, just like you, and worked my tail off to make it come true—but I didn't do it alone. I had a lot of help. I was also blessed with an opportunity to build something special (more than once). How fortunate is that? So many people never even get one great opportunity in life! So I know I have been fortunate, and I thank my lucky stars every day for that.

But being thankful is not enough. You have to channel that gratitude into tangible, positive actions if you want to max out your potential in this lifetime.

I'm telling you—good karma is worth a trillion dollars.

One way I like to show my gratitude is to pay it forward, passing down what I have learned about being an entrepreneur. I do it every time I meet a young entrepreneur in real life, and I am doing it now in the pages of this book.

I don't want to get too New Agey or metaphysical on you, but I believe every generation is connected. As much as we think we live and die alone in this world, we are all part of the same dance. So for all of us "silver foxes" out there who are nearing retirement age, sharing what we have learned with other people is one way we can help make life easier for future generations.

I learned the 101 lessons in this book, some might say, the hard way. I sure as heck did not learn them from any book! Maybe you will take them to heart—and maybe you won't and will still have to learn them the hard way. Whatever path you choose, I feel like I have done my small part to get you headed in the right direction.

Now, like I said, the choice is entirely up to you . . .

WHEN YOU CAN GIVE BACK, DO IT ANY WAY YOU CAN

I know I've spent most of the time talking about business and not nearly enough time talking about the "business of giving back." This is a real thing, guys and gals: they call it philanthropy!

Don't forget to be philanthropic. Nothing feels better than putting a lot of blood, sweat, and tears into making a good living—then being able to give some of it back to people who are less fortunate than you. This is not just a tax write-off I'm talking about here. This is no obligation. This is a privilege. When you hit it big—and I know all of you will—find a way to give something back, one way or another.

Some people make donations, while others donate their time. Still others donate their money and time. Whenever I can, that's what I choose to do . . . both. That said, there is also a fourth way to give back that truly is the best of all. What am I talking about?

I'm talking about building a socially conscious business. The best example of this (I know of) came from my good friend Jeff Brown. He is a very successful owner of thirteen supermarkets in Philadelphia, which is no big deal, right? Well, it gets better. Jeff decided to open eight of his supermarkets in some of the most impoverished neighborhoods in Philadelphia. These neighborhoods were like war zones that the other supermarket companies abandoned more than twenty years ago. Not Jeff. His markets have given these neighborhoods a place to get nutritious food, health services, and (just as important) hundreds of new jobs.

What a great idea!

Jeff's supermarkets have not only made a huge impact in those neighborhoods, but he also created a successful philanthropic business model for others to follow. His supermarkets became such a big deal, President Obama "tipped his cap" to Jeff in his 2010 State of the Union Address; Jeff was even invited to travel to DC to sit next to Michelle Obama during the speech!

Now that's what I'm talking about.

Jeff came up with a bold way to use his business to give something back to eight communities that needed help—and do some good in this world. And it's still paying dividends to this day. Not only in dollars but in karma bucks!

And that's what we all want to do, right? Rack up those karma bucks?

It took me a few years to realize that life is not all about stacking dollars to the ceiling and flying around in private jets. It's about making the world a better place than when we found it. It may not always be possible to change the world, but you can always pull your weight. So whenever you get a chance, get to pulling already!

Your karma will thank you.

HE WHO WORKS THE HARDEST
USUALLY WINS

One thing that helped me be successful in life was that my parents instilled a no-nonsense work ethic in me that I hope you have lurking somewhere in your arsenal as well. I've noticed very few people these days seem to have it embedded in their DNA, unless some authority figure took the time to drum it into them. For me, that person was not Marty—it was my mom, if you can believe that.

Thanks, Mom!

I remember she was extremely fastidious about her gardens and lawn; they had to be perfect. She never thought of hiring a gardener. That just wasn't her style. So when I was a kid and wanted to go play basketball in the summer—guess what? I had to finish my chores before I could go have any fun. I still remember all those hot summer mornings when I was outside cutting the grass or picking the weeds out of the garden. I would be cursing my mother under my breath while my friends were already out playing hoops next door.

Talk about learning work-life balance! I wasn't having fun picking weeds or mowing the lawn at the time—that's why they call it "tough love"—but Mom taught me a valuable lesson that I still live by today.

Get your work done before you go play!

Don't celebrate like you just won the championship after you made your first shot! Focus on doing a great job at what you are doing right now, in the present tense. And don't be afraid to put in the elbow grease!

I realize it's nearly impossible to get this across to you now, when you are an adult. I hope you had someone who cared enough about you to instill that same no-nonsense work ethic in you when you were younger.

And if you did, find a moment to thank them, because you are sure as heck going to need a killer work ethic if you want to get this idea of yours off the ground and into the big time.

Remember, "He who works the hardest, usually wins . . . "

ONE FINAL CALL TO ACTION

Well, here we are. I'm not going to be around after you close this book and go off to turn your big idea into a startup business. You're on your own! I do hope you will take my 101 lessons to heart. You may not be able to afford Harvard Business School (who can these days?), but at least now you have a course from Coach Green that will help you thrive on the business court.

I'm not going to sit here and tell you that achieving your dream is going to be effortless—it's not. It's going to be the hardest thing you'll ever do. But it just might be the most rewarding thing you ever do, too.

Will you become the next Bill Gates or Elon Musk?

Maybe . . . but (hey), I didn't even become those guys! But I still had a pretty good life, and you can too. You're so much farther ahead of the game than most aspiring entrepreneurs are. Why?

You already have a passion!

You already have a big idea!

And you have the ambition to make it reality.

Do you know how many people slog through life never finding their passion? So many settle for what's right in front of them and never dare to even dream.

That's not you, and that's not me. So don't listen to the naysayers. Never let someone convince you that you should lower your expectations, and never ever give up on your dreams.

Can you do this thing?

It's entirely up to you. No outcomes are guaranteed in life. All you can do is put yourself in a position to win, work your tail off, and trust that the universe will meet you halfway (like it did me).

If it's fated, it will happen.

Don't tighten up now.

Need some inspiration? Want to hear one of my favorite quotes of all time? It came from a guy who had the heart and soul of a thousand men. His name was Jim Valvano, and he was the basketball coach of North Carolina State University for many years. I was not lucky enough to meet him personally, but I remember when Jim got up to speak at the 1993 ESPY Awards. He made an amazing speech eight weeks before he died of bone cancer. For me, one of his most memorable "calls to action" was:

There are 86,400 seconds in a day.
It's up to you to decide what to do with them . . .

Did you see that? Another second just ticked by . . . then another . . . and another.

Think of all those untapped seconds!

The question is: what are you going to do with them?

If you take control of your seconds, you will really be taking control of the rest of your life. That's the real message I've tried to share with you in these pages. Take control, live life to the fullest, learn from your own mistakes, and by all means learn from mine.

At the same time, I hope that many if not most of the 101 lessons I've sought to teach in this book go straight to your heart. They say that it's easier, faster, and cheaper to learn from the experience of others. I've poured many of my experiences into this book with the goal of making you a happier, more successful businessperson.

So now go out and knock 'em dead, and when you and your family are enjoying that better life you've created for them, send me a note and tell me about it!

Acknowledgments

I want to take this opportunity to acknowledge and appreciate my amiable and supportive wife, Amy. I make bold to say that marrying you has been the best decision I have ever made in my entire life. Amy, you have always been there to keep me centered and provide strength whenever I was weak. My wife is my love, confidant, and top advisor. I couldn't have asked for a better life partner. You, Amy, are the best!

My work is important to me but my family is my inspiration. To my children: Allison, her husband Brian, Laura, her husband Alec, and Adam, I say a big thank you for being a part of my world. You've been a constant source of motivation for me to excel and have unconsciously pushed me to maximize my potentials. I am grateful for your words of encouragement and the support you offer me. Keep being awesome. You rock! I love you all!

I saved the most precious thing in my life for last, my granddaughters Emma and Lexie. I look forward to the day when you can read and understand more about me. That makes me feel wonderful. Remember, be all that you can be. Furthermore, I would like to say thank you to all of my future grandchildren for enlightening my life with your innocence and pureness. I don't know you yet, but I already love you!